THE HEALING
ENIGMA

*The Physician-Priest
in the 21st Century*

Dr Robert M Jaggs-Fowler

CStJ MBBS LLM MA FRCGP FRSA

Copyright © 2018 Robert Jaggs-Fowler

The moral right of the author has been asserted.

Apart from any fair dealing for the purposes of research or private study, or criticism or review, as permitted under the Copyright, Designs and Patents Act 1988, this publication may only be reproduced, stored or transmitted, in any form or by any means, with the prior permission in writing of the publishers, or in the case of reprographic reproduction in accordance with the terms of licences issued by the Copyright Licensing Agency. Enquiries concerning reproduction outside those terms should be sent to the publishers.

Matador
9 Priory Business Park,
Wistow Road, Kibworth Beauchamp,
Leicestershire. LE8 0RX
Tel: 0116 279 2299
Email: books@troubador.co.uk
Web: www.troubador.co.uk/matador
Twitter: @matadorbooks

ISBN 978 1789015 393

British Library Cataloguing in Publication Data.
A catalogue record for this book is available from the British Library.

Printed and bound in the UK by TJ International, Padstow, Cornwall
Typeset in 11pt Aldine by Troubador Publishing Ltd, Leicester, UK

Matador is an imprint of Troubador Publishing Ltd

To my late father,
Robert John Lawrence Fowler,
whose personal search for meaning and understanding
of life has persistently fuelled my lifetime of endeavour.
I am the man of his child.

ALSO BY
ROBERT JAGGS-FOWLER

Fiction
Lamplight in the Shadows

Poetry
On Quarry Beach
A Journey with Time

Non-fiction
The Law and Medicine:
Friend or Nemesis?

Contents

Preface		vii
About the Author		ix
Acknowledgements		xi
Introduction		xiii
I	Historical, Cultural and Multi-faith Perspectives	1
II	The Christian Perspective	13
III	Modern-Day Perspectives	28
IV	The Future Perspective	44
Conclusion		57
Bibliography		63

Preface

The role of the priest-physician has existed from pre-Christian times and historic reference to such a person can be found within the majority of religions and across all continents. Christianity is a religion of healing, the evidence for which can be found throughout the New Testament. Christ fulfilled the roles of both priest and physician, and St Luke might be seen as the first Christian physician-priest. However, despite the significant role Christianity has played in the development of modern-day health services, and despite the growing body of scientific evidence indicating the value of spirituality and religion in respect to the maintenance of good health and increased recovery from illness, the 20th century medical profession within the Western world placed religion at arm's length, and officially and effectively excluded such discussion from the medical consultation.

Through a search of primary and secondary sources within theological, medical, legal, historic and philosophical literature, an argument has been formed in support of a 21st century role for the 'physician-priest', whereby the physician can exercise the role of priest in addition to the medical role, and thereby truly minister to the whole person in terms of mind, body and soul.

With consideration of modern NHS funding streams, a radical proposal is suggested, whereby the Church of England and medical educational institutions might combine to offer dual theological and medical training; thus, establishing a new breed of professional person ideally positioned in respect to the care of the elderly and those with terminal illness. It is suggested that this not only assists with the provision of 'whole-person' care but allows the Church to firmly re-establish itself in the 21st century within its Christian healing tradition.

Robert M Jaggs-Fowler
Barton upon Humber
Petertide, 2018

About the Author

Dr Robert M Jaggs-Fowler, a Kentish Man by birth, is an ordinand, physician, writer and poet who divides his time between Lincolnshire, North Yorkshire and Cyprus. With Medical degrees, a Master of Laws degree in Medical Law and Ethics, and a Master of Arts degree in Spirituality, Theology and Health, he is currently researching a theology PhD thesis at Durham University, whilst completing his final year of ministerial training at the Lincoln School of Theology.

A former GP, Medical Director and Director of Primary Care for the NHS North Lincolnshire Clinical Commissioning Group, Robert is a Commander of the Most Venerable Order of the Hospital of St John of Jerusalem, a former Major in the Royal Army Medical Corps, and a Fellow of the Royal Society of Arts. He is Liveryman in the Worshipful Society of Apothecaries and holds the Freedom of the City of London.

Robert is the author of several books, a former columnist for two regional newspapers and a county magazine, has had several short stories, non-fiction and 'filler' articles published, was a regular contributor to an American travel website, and contributed to an American film script. He won the Lincoln Book Festival Prize for fiction in 2005 and the Fathom Prize for poetry in 2010.

Acknowledgements

I am indebted to the many organisations and the numerous, and often anonymous, individuals who willingly offered assistance during the preparation of this book. The exclusion of any person or establishment from this list is an error of personal oversight, for which I apologise.

In particular, I am grateful to the Librarian and staff of the Bill Bryson Library at Durham University, the Librarian of the Royal College of General Practitioners, and the staff of the British Library, London. I am also beholden to all the academics and authors whose original work has been the fuel to inspire my own thinking. It is hoped that I have given appropriate acknowledgement of all such sources within the text and bibliography and have avoided any inadvertent breaches of copyright. I apologise for any possible errors in this respect.

Finally, but by no means least importantly, I wish to acknowledge with gratitude the patience and guidance of The Reverend Professor Christopher C H Cook, BSc MB BS MD MA PhD FRCPsych, of the Department of Theology and Religion at Durham University, whose objective views, suggestions and encouragement were most valuable. Any deficiencies remain of my own making.

Introduction

*We are not human beings having a spiritual experience;
we are spiritual beings having a human experience.*[1]

Pierre Teilhard de Chardin (1881–1955)

For many living within what is widely acknowledged to be an increasingly secular society, the idea of even considering that there might be a role for a physician-priest within the 21st century will be anathema. Even the idea that the two roles might possibly be entwined will be an alien concept. However, it has not always been the case, and within many ancient texts the priest-physician is a common trope. For some societies (albeit not necessarily Christian ones), the dual role of priest-physician, remains the norm. The concept of the physician-priest, as opposed to the priest-physician, is merely a difference in emphasis on the primary occupation.

Amongst Western medicine, there is a valid argument to suggest that truly holistic care cannot be achieved by divorcing mental health from physical health, and as an extension to that, the separation of spiritual health from

---

1   Robert J. Furey, *The Joy of Kindness* (New York: Crossroad Publishing Co., 1993), p. 138.

mental health is equally nonsensical. Here, the term spiritual is used to encapsulate all aspects of spirituality, religion and faith of all persuasions and of none; for it can also be argued that there is no such thing as the non-spiritual person. The perceptive insight attributed to Pierre Teilhard de Chardin, that 'we are not human beings having a spiritual experience; we are spiritual beings having a human experience', succinctly and aptly summarises this.

Within the medical profession, the general medical practitioner (GP) is arguably more likely to consider the holistic care of a patient than many of his or her specialised colleagues, for that is a central tenet of the training; and amongst the latter, it is likely to be the psychiatrist who will more readily recognise the spiritual impact on a patient's well-being. For these reasons, this dissertation has been written with these two professional groups specifically in mind.

However, despite the above, secular organisations within society in general, and the medical regulatory bodies such as the General Medical Council in particular, have not always been supportive of extending the 'holistic care' concept to a spiritual or religious dimension within the setting of the medical consultation. This has made many physicians wary of treading on such ground for fear of public and professional opprobrium, or worse, a loss of their licence to practise medicine.

Nonetheless, there is also a body of opinion that would suggest that, within modern times, the physician has gradually replaced the parish priest in respect to whom a person consults over many non-medical issues. There is also a train of thought suggesting that many aspects of the routine clinical examination (for example, the auscultation of a chest with a stethoscope, or the palpation of the abdomen) are in themselves ritualistic[2] and, as such, have a therapeutic component to them, just as kneeling in prayer or receiving a blessing accompanied by the sign of the cross may have in the religious setting.

So, in essence, the question arises as to whether there is such a difference between the two roles of priest and physician or, apart from the obvious difference in regards to their respective knowledge bases, whether a significant component of the two roles overlaps. This has most certainly been recognised by many physicians who, at some stage of their working lives, have either functioned separately as a clinician during the week and as a part-time priest at weekends, or sought ordination after their retirement from clinical practice.

This dissertation examines this concept, by considering the historical background to the two professions, reflecting on the individual roles of priests and physicians, studying the theology of healing, and ultimately asking what is the role of a dually-qualified person – a physician-priest – in the 21st century?

---

[2] John S. Welch, 'Ritual in Western Medicine and Its Role in Placebo Healing', *Journal of Religion and Health*, 42, no. 1, (2003), 21–33.

I

Historical, Cultural and Multi-faith Perspectives

A physician who is at the same time a philosopher is like a god.
The Hippocratic Corpus[3]

Consideration of the role of the 'physician-priest' in the 21st century needs to be taken within the context of the historic development of medicine in general, and the role of religion in respect to that development in particular. It is a journey that is both evolutionary in societal and scholastic terms, as well as providing an evidential platform of some considerable substance with which to support the argument for the existence of theological authenticity for such a role within the modern era.

Within prehistoric times, and up to about 600 BC, the 'medicine-man' fulfilled the combined roles of physician, priest and magician.[4] A specific version, found even today amongst Eskimos, Siberian and some African

---

3 Elizabeth M. Craik, *The Hippocratic Corpus: Content and Context* (London: Routledge, 2015), p. 57.
4 Kurt Pollak, *The Healers: The Doctor, Then and Now* (London: Thomas Nelson & Sons, 1963), p. 6.

tribes, was the shaman; a person who had some form of mental illness at the time of puberty, and then progressed to the status of a priest-physician.

Prior to the advent of scientific medicine, and most certainly prior to Hippocrates, advice, instruction and laws regarding health matters and rituals of healing were predominantly found in religious texts.[5] Within such manuscripts, there is ample evidence to support the understanding that the priests of that era were also responsible for health matters. Indeed, the area known as the ancient Near East (Babylonia, Egypt, Mesopotamia and Syria) most certainly combined healing with theology, and many texts contain reference to the 'priest-physician'.[6] In Mesopotamia, at the time of Hammurabi, King of Babylon (c.1810–1750 BC), the Asu (who practised primitive pharmacy and surgery) became more independent of the priesthood and practised medicine and surgery under the Code of Hammurabi,[7] [8] [9] albeit whilst calling upon the services of the god Nabu, whose knowledge of all sciences and medicine was pre-eminent.[10] The Egyptian priest Imhotep (c. 2650–2600 BC) is the first person to be identified as a physician

---

5 Robert Jaggs-Fowler, *The Law and Medicine: Friend or Nemesis?* (London: Radcliffe Publishing, 2013), p. 27.
6 William Bynum, *The History of Medicine: A Very Short Introduction* (Oxford: Oxford University Press, 2008), p. 7.
7 Pollak, p. 14.
8 Roberto Margotta, *History of Medicine* (London: Octobus Publishing, [1996] 2001), p. 10.
9 The first code to delineate the civil and criminal liabilities of the medical profession.
10 Pollak, p. 16.

within known history[11] (although the evidence that he was actually a physician is disputed).[12] Later immortalised as a god, after his death, Imhotep was subsequently adopted by the Greeks as their healing god, Asclepius,[13] though the temple sanctuary of Imhotep continued to be used by priest-physicians to assist the ailments of pilgrims up to at least the 4th century AD.[14]

Even at the time of Hippocrates (widely considered to be the father of scientific medicine), the Greeks had many temples dedicated to Asclepius. These temples were served by resident priests, whom people consulted in respect to various ailments. The priests made their diagnoses by interpreting patients' dreams, aided in some manner by holy snakes (which in turn became part of the caduceus – the staff and snake, symbolic of Asclepius). Other temples were dedicated to the daughters of Asclepius, namely Hygieia and Panacea, who were the goddesses of hygiene and healing respectively.[15]

Within India, the oldest pieces of literature are the sacred Sanskrit books known as the four Vedas (written in the second millennium BC).[16] Of these, the *Ayurveda* (which translates as 'The Art of Life'), is the one that

---

11   Ibid., p. 19.
12   Plinio Prioreschi, *A History of Medicine* (Omaha: Horatius Press, 1995), p. 357.
13   Pollak, p. 19.
14   Ibid., p. 20.
15   Arthur K. Shapiro and Elaine Shapiro, *The Powerful Placebo: From Ancient Priest to Modern Physician* (Baltimore: The John Hopkins University Press, 1997), pp. 5–6.
16   S. Jain and P. N. Tandon, 'Ayurvedic medicine and Indian literature on epilepsy', *Neurology Asia*, 9, Supplement 1 (2004), 57–58.

relates most to the practise of medicine.[17] Through the *Ayurveda*, it was considered that healing is a power passed from heaven to the demigods, and thence to priests, some of whom specialised in the practise of healing. This is still the case in many parts of India, as the authority of the Vedas is recognised by Hindus within what is collectively known as Hinduism.[18]

It is recognised that, within most of these cultures, and most certainly in the Egyptian and Indian cultures, the priest-physicians were powerfully placed in society and held significant social esteem.[19] [20] In Indian society, this was the case until about 200 BC, when the orthodox priests began to distance themselves from priest-physicians on the grounds that they were unclean; thus, resulting in them being barred from participating in sacred rituals. This subsequently became Hindu Law[21] and represented a major shift in the development of the Indian medical profession. However, it has also been claimed that the advances in knowledge in respect to medicine and surgery also enabled medicine to 'escape the hands of the priests'.[22]

In Japan, Buddhism was introduced in the sixth century AD, and from then until 1869 it was the

---

17 Kenneth Zysk, 'Mythology and the brahmanization of Indian medicine: transforming heterodoxy into orthodoxy', www.hindu.dk, <http://www.hindu.dk/4/ar/zysk2.pdf> [accessed 07 March 2015].
18 Ninian Smart, *The World's Religions* (Cambridge: Cambridge University Press, 1989), p. 53.
19 Pollak, p. 25.
20 Zysk, 'Mythology and the brahmanization of Indian medicine'.
21 G. Buhler (trans.), 'Manusmrti: The Laws of Manu', <http://sanskritdocuments.org/all_pdf/manusmriti.pdf> [accessed 07 March 2015].
22 Pollak, p. 32.

Buddhist priests who provided medical care.[23] Indeed, when Japan started to send diplomatic missions to the Sui and Tang courts of China (607–894 AD), four fifths were priest-physicians.[24]

The historical situation on the American continent was not much different from that of Europe, Asia and Africa. In Central America, the Maya population (commencing 2000 BC) also had priest-physicians, who practised in accordance with their belief in the cyclical nature of time and life; that being the basis of their pre-Columbian religion.[25] Similarly, in the Aztec (c.1250–1521 AD) and Inca (13th century–1572 AD) civilisations, it was the priests who had access to knowledge and thus, not surprisingly, the physicians were in the class of priests.[26]

Within the Abrahamic faiths,[27] both health care and medical treatments appear within the Old Testament; a good example being the Book of Leviticus. The latter is the third book of the Hebrew Bible (i.e. the Old Testament)[28] and was later incorporated into the Jewish Torah (c.55–400 BC).[29] Leviticus is forthright in respect to the laws governing health, cleanliness, the performance of

---

23 Edward R. Drott, 'Gods, Buddhas, and Organs: Buddhist Physicians and Theories of Longevity in Early Medieval Japan', *Japanese Journal of Religious Studies*, 37, no. 2 (2010), 247–73.

24 Ibid.

25 Francisco Guerra, 'Maya Medicine', *Medical History*, 8 (1964), pp. 31–43.

26 Charles Coury, 'The Basic Principles of Medicine in the Primitive Mind', *Medical History*, 11 (1967), pp. 111–127.

27 Judaism, Christianity and Islam.

28 *The Holy Bible*, New Revised Standard Version, Anglicized Edition (Oxford: Oxford University Press, 1995).

29 *The Jewish Study Bible*, ed. by Adele Berlin and Marc Zvi Brettler (Oxford: Oxford University Press, 2004).

circumcision, the treatment of leprosy, and the manner in which blood, semen and pus should be dealt with.[30] The Qur'an,[31] the main religious text of Islam, continues the emphasis on maintaining good health, but has little to say on the subject of medical treatments.[32]

Compared to many other religions and cultures described above, the direct interconnection of the role of priests and physicians is slightly harder to demonstrate within Judaism. However, whilst it is the case that a rabbi is not a priest, whether in the Jewish or Christian sense of the word (as a priest has special authority to act out certain sacred rituals and rabbis have no greater authority in this regard than any adult Jewish male), rabbis are still highly esteemed religious figures within Jewish communities. It is therefore considered appropriate to mention here one rabbi who is pre-eminent amongst medical persons in the history of Judaism. That is Moshe ben Maimon, otherwise known as Maimonides (c.1135–1204).[33] Maimonides was a physician as well as a rabbi, and an influential Torah scholar.[34] [35] It is to Maimonides that the 'Physician's Prayer' is attributed (albeit possibly erroneously).[36]

---

30 Lev. 11–16.
31 *The Koran*, trans. by J. M. Rodwell, (London: Phoenix, 1909).
32 F. Rahman, 'Islam and Health/Medicine: A historical perspective', in: *Healing and Restoring: Health and Medicine in the World's Religious Traditions*, ed. by L. E. Sullivan, (New York: Macmillan Publishing Co., 1989), p. 154.
33 Joel L. Kraemer, *Maimonides: The Life and World of one of Civilisation's Greatest Minds* (New York: Doubleday Religion, 2010), p. 1.
34 Maimonides compiled the 'Thirteen Articles'; the principles of belief that form the basis of the Jewish Creed.
35 Arthur Hyman, 'Maimonides' "Thirteen Principles"', *Jewish Medieval and Renaissance Studies*, (1967), 119–144.
36 Leonard Wexler, 'The Prayer of Maimonides', *Oncology Times*, 31, no. 4 (2009), 3.

It can be safely said that Christianity revolutionised the care of the sick throughout its spheres of influence in the world. Apart from the scriptural teachings on the matter of healing, the monastic orders in particular were instrumental in introducing and providing healthcare and hospitals. For example, during the medieval period, many Benedictine monasteries had hospital facilities in accordance with St Benedict's Rule stating that 'care of the sick must rank above and before all else'.[37] This Christian perspective is discussed in greater detail in Chapter II.

During medieval times in the Greek Church, it was common for distinguished laymen to be ordained as priests, and this included physicians.[38] The latter then served as 'physician-priests', looking after the spiritual as well as physical health of the population, which marked a reversal of the earlier trend for priests to train in medicine and thus become 'priest-physicians'. It was even known for physicians to be ordained as bishops and thus become 'physician-bishops'.[39] Theodotos, Bishop of Laodicea, is one such example[40] and is known to have attended the first council of Nicea[41] [42] in 325 AD.[43] Even

---

37 *The Rule of St Benedict in English,* ed. by Timothy Fry (Collegeville: The Liturgical Press, 1981), p. 59.
38 Demetrios J. Constantelos, 'Physician-Priests in the Medieval Greek Church', *Greek Orthodox Theological Review,* 11 (1966), 141–53.
39 Ibid.
40 Ibid.
41 The Council of Nicea was the first ecumenical council, at which it was affirmed that Jesus was 'of one substance' with the Father, and from which the Nicene Creed originated.
42 Alister E. McGrath, *Christian Theology: An Introduction* (Chichester: Wiley-Blackwell, 2011), p. 17.
43 Joannes Dominicus Mansi, *Sacrorum Conciliorum Nova et Amplissima Collectio,* vol. 2 (1692-1769) col. 693D, < http://www.

into the late sixth and early seventh centuries, physician-bishops still existed. Indeed, in 768 AD a physician-priest was appointed as Patriarch of Alexandria (the highest ranking Greek Orthodox bishop of Egypt).[44] In 1276, this was matched in Western Europe when a Portuguese physician called Peter Juliani was elected Bishop of Rome and became Pope John XXI.[45]

Somewhat ironically, in light of the General Medical Council's 21st century stance against physicians discussing religion in the consulting room (*vide infra*), sometime between 1157–1169 an encyclical was issued by Patriarch Lukas Chrysoberges that prevented Greek Orthodox priests from practising medicine on the grounds that it was 'improper';[46] although it is known that the practice actually continued into the 16th and 17th centuries.[47] This prohibition was echoed in the Western Christian Church in 1163 (when monks were prevented from attending medical lectures), and followed through in 1215 when the Fourth Lateran Council banned the practising of surgery by the higher orders of clergy (deacons, priests and bishops). In the late 15th century, the pressure against the study of medicine escalated, with clergy and their medical teachers being threatened with excommunication.[48]

---

documentacatholicaomnia.eu/01_50_1692-1769-_Mansi_JD.html> [accessed 13 March 2015].
44   Demetrios J. Constantelos.
45   Johann Peter Kirsch, 'Pope John XXI (XX)', in: *The Catholic Encyclopaedia* (New York: Robert Appleton Company, 1910), <http://www.newadvent.org/cathen/08429c.htm> [accessed 14 March 2015].
46   Ibid.
47   Ibid.
48   Pollak, p. 32.

Nonetheless, the story does not end there. Within the second half of the 16th century, the Protestant reformist John Calvin[49] wrote of the significant role for deacons in respect to the spiritual care of sick people as well as the treatment of their physical diseases.[50] Thereby bringing the connection between religion and medicine firmly back into at least one formulation of religious doctrine, albeit not specifically as 'priest-physicians'. In respect to diaconal ministry in the Church of England today, the emphasis on the pastoral role of deacons in respect to the sick continues to be part of the service of ordination (*vide infra*).[51] [52]

Similarly to Christianity, Islam has been responsible for significant developments in modern medicine through its quest for knowledge, developing technologies and founding of medical schools and hospitals.[53] Indeed, *Avicenna's Canon of Medicine*[54] was once a foundational text in many traditional Islamic seminaries, and there is substantial literature in the field of *al-tibb al-Nabawi*

---

49 Mary E. Coleman, 'John Calvin (1509–64)', in: *The Student's Companion to the Theologians*, ed. by Ian S. Markham (Chichester: Wiley-Blackwell, 2013), pp. 199–203.
50 *The Task of Healing: Medicine, Religion, and Gender in England and the Netherlands, 1450–1800*, ed. by H. Marland and M. Pelling (Rotterdam: Erasmus Publishing, 1996), p. 155.
51 Martin Davie, *A Guide To The Church of England* (London: Bloomsbury, 2008), pp. 112–13.
52 Church of England, *Common Worship: Services and Prayers for the Church of England: Ordination Services* (London: Church House Publishing, 2007), p. 15.
53 Azeem Majeed, 'How Islam changed medicine', *BMJ*, 331 (2005), 1486-7.
54 Ibn Sīnā (Avicenna), *Al-Qānūn fī al-Ṭibb* (*The Canon of Medicine*) (c. 1025), <http://archive.org/stream/AvicennasCanonOfMedicine/9670940-Canon-of-Medicine_djvu.txt> [accessed 30 March 2015].

(Prophetic Medicine);[55] reflective of Islam's concept of the mind, body and spirit representing a single unity. However, whilst Islam 'recognises medicine as an allowable and necessary profession',[56] there is a paucity of research on the active role of the imam in respect to health care.[57] [58] Important potential roles for imams in respect to health care have been identified, namely:

1) encouraging healthy behaviours through scripture-based messages in sermons;
2) performing religious rituals around life events and illnesses;
3) advocating for Muslim patients and delivering cultural sensitivity training in hospitals;
4) assisting in healthcare decisions for Muslims.[59]

However, it is equally true to state that Islamic hospitals have historically been under secular control.[60] Indeed, a literature search found nothing to suggest the historic or present existence of a dually qualified imam-physician,

---

55 Ibrahim Amin, Imam and theologian, Oxford Centre for Islamic Studies, University of Oxford (personal correspondence, March 2015).
56 S. Taavoni, 'Only a nice man can be a nice physician', *Iran Journal of Nursing*, 13, no. 21 (1999), 42–45.
57 Aasim I. Padela and others, 'Health: Perspectives of Muslim Community Leaders in Southeast Michigan', *Journal of Religion and Health,* 50, no. 2 (2011), 359–73.
58 Ibid.
59 Amin states that there are a number of 'potential Imams' who have theological training but now pursue alternative vocations including medicine. However, no research has focused on this group (personal correspondence, March 2015).
60 Sami Hamarneh, 'Development of Hospitals in Islam', *Journal of the History of Medicine and Allied Sciences,* 17, no. 3 (1962), 366–84.

and this may be owing to some Muslim behaviours and Islamic ethics being a barrier to good health care (for example, fasting during Ramadan and issues regarding permitted therapeutics),[61] thereby making the two roles not entirely compatible for one person to undertake. It has also been suggested that the role of the imam is often intensive, with the daily cycle of five prayers and other educational responsibilities within the community precluding the possibility of pursuing an additional or combined vocation.[62] The absence of a church in Islam[63] also means that no Muslim has a sacramental office; in other words, the Muslim equivalent of the Christian priest does not exist and thus, *ipso facto*, neither can there be the Islamic equivalent of the priest-physician.

Summary

It can be safely stated that, from the time human civilisation started to have a recorded history, there has been a very close relationship between religion and medicine.[64] Indeed, it is difficult not to assume that the same was the case before the start of written records. This relationship almost inevitably meant that those who studied medicine were likely also to be priests, as it was

---

61 Aasim I. Padela, 'Health: Perspectives of Muslim Community Leaders in Southeast Michigan'.
62 Ibrahim Amin.
63 Malise Ruthven, *Islam: A Very Short Introduction* (Oxford: Oxford University Press, 2012), p. 74.
64 S Chattopadhyay, 'Religion, spirituality, health and medicine: Why should Indian physicians care?', *Journal of Postgraduate Medicine*, 53, no. 4 (2007), 262–66.

predominantly the priests who had access to knowledge and were thus educated. Hence, the 'priest-physician' or 'priest-doctor' became common tropes throughout early history; the concept fitting well with John of Damascus's idea that human beings are 'psycho-somatic entities'.[65] What is more, this was a universal situation, being found across all continents and in all religions, with the one possible exception of Islam.

Yet, despite the advancement of science within the late 19th, 20th and early 21st centuries, with all the pharmacological armoury at the disposal of modern civilisations and the myriad of investigative processes, the physician is still held by many as someone with exalted powers; an image that directly connects the 21st century physician with his or her counterpart in pre-history. As Calder acknowledged, the reputation of today's physicians is still underpinned by folk mythology, including that of priest-physicians of old, sages, and practitioners of alchemy.[66]

---

65 John Damascenos, *De Fide Orthodoxa*, Bk.II, ch. XII (650-754 AD), <http://www.documentacatholicaomnia.eu/03d/0675-0749,_Ioannes_Damascenus,_De_Fide_Orthodoxa,_EN.pdf> [accessed 13 March 2015].
66 R. Calder, *From Magic to Medicine* (London: Rathbone Books, 1957), pp. 6–7.

II

The Christian Perspective

Then Jesus went about all the cities and villages, teaching in their synagogues, and proclaiming the good news of the kingdom, and curing every disease and every sickness.

Matthew 9.35

Christ as Priest and Healer

Placing aside for one moment matters of theology, the question as to 'who was Jesus?' is one scholars have debated since the earliest records of Christianity. Indeed, it is still a question to which historians often find themselves at odds with each other.[67] However, regardless of the paucity of detail regarding the early life of Jesus, or the fact that the earliest known writings about his life were started some years after his crucifixion,[68] [69] the fact remains that, apart from any question of Jesus's divinity,

---

67 David Boulton, *Who on Earth was Jesus?* (Winchester: O Books, 2008), xvi.
68 Ibid., p. 40.
69 Paul's letters are thought to have been written around 50 AD, Mark's gospel in the 70s, Matthew's gospel in the 80s, Luke's account in the late 80s to early 90s, and John completed his in the early 1st century.

there is a heavy emphasis within the New Testament on his work as a healer. Indeed, it is true to say that, at its heart, Christianity is a religion of healing;[70] as witnessed not only by the gospels, but by the role of Christianity in the development of health care in general and monastically governed hospitals, in particular during the Medieval period.[71] Even today, within the early 21st century, there are some who hold the view that 'a Christian can never discuss healing without having Jesus in mind'.[72]

The gospel of Mark, in particular, is rich with reference to the healing power of Jesus. Examples include the stopping of a man's convulsions,[73] [74] the arresting of a woman's haemorrhage,[75] the raising of a young girl from death,[76] the curing of a paralyzed man,[77] and the curing of leprosy,[78] to name but a few. The other gospel writers add to these examples, including the healing of an impotent man,[79] the restoration of a withered hand,[80] the restoration of sight to two men,[81]

---

70   Amanda Porterfield, *Healing in the History of Christianity* (Oxford: Oxford University Press, 2005), pp. 44–45.
71   Alister E. McGrath, 'Christianity', in: *Oxford Textbook of Spirituality in Healthcare*, ed. by Mark Cobb, Christina M. Puchalski and Bruce Rumbold (Oxford: Oxford University Press, 2012), pp. 25–30.
72   Morris Maddocks, *The Christian Healing Ministry*, 3rd edn (London: SPCK, [1981] 1995), p. 9.
73   Mk 1.24.
74   Mk 9.17–18.
75   Mk 6.56.
76   Mk 5.41.
77   Mk 2.8–12.
78   Mk 1.40–42.
79   Jn 5.1–16.
80   Mt. 12.9–13.
81   Mt. 20.29–34.

and the healing of Malchus's ear.[82] In respect to these, and whilst defending himself against criticism from the scribes of the Pharisees, Jesus at one stage implies that he sees himself as a form of physician:

Those who are well have no need of a physician, but I have come to call not the righteous but sinners.[83]

It is true that, in this particular incident, he was using an analogy to demonstrate his purpose for keeping company with tax collectors and other so-called 'sinners'; but nonetheless, the inference is also there that he saw himself as a person whose role was to make people better. It is suggested, therefore, that he may well have likened himself to a physician, i.e. 'one who practices the healing art';[84] but a physician whose powers were a gift from God rather than a qualification bestowed by humankind.

However, healer or physician aside, Christian doctrine derived predominantly from the Old Testament also maintains that Jesus also had the *munus triplex* (threefold mission) of prophet,[85][86][87] priest[88][89][90] and King.[91][92] It is a doctrine first described by the 4th century

---

82 Lk. 22.49–51.
83 Mk 2.17.
84 *Butterworths Medical Dictionary*, ed. by Macdonald Critchley, 2nd edn (London: Butterworths, [1961] 1978).
85 Deuteronomy 18.14–22.
86 Mt. 21.11.
87 Lk. 4.24.
88 Heb. 9.12.
89 Heb. 7.25.
90 Ps. 110.1–4.
91 Ps. 2.
92 Jn 18.36.

theologian, Eusebius, who wrote:

> *...all these have reference to the true Christ, the divinely inspired and heavenly Word, who is the only high priest of all, and the only King of every creature, and the Father's only supreme prophet of prophets.*[93]

This was further expanded by the theologian, John Calvin, who wrote:

> *Therefore, in order that faith may find a firm basis for salvation in Christ, and thus rest in him, this principle must be laid down: the office enjoined upon Christ by the Father consists of three parts. For he was given to be prophet, king and priest.*[94]

Of the three facets of the *munus triplex*, it is the role of priest that is of specific interest here. According to the Westminster Shorter Catechism,[95] Jesus fulfils the role of priest by:

> *offering up of himself as a sacrifice to satisfy divine justice,*[96]
> *reconciling us to God,*[97]
> *in making continual intercession for us.*[98]

---

[93] Eusebius, *Ecclesiastical History* (*circa* 340 AD) Bk. 1, Chp. 3, Para. 8 <http://www.documentacatholicaomnia.eu/03d/0265-0339,_Eusebius_Caesariensis,_Church_History,_EN.pdf> [accessed 11 April 2015].

[94] John Calvin, *The Institutes of the Christian Religion* (1536) *Bk.* II, Chp. 15, p. 305, trans. by Henry Beveridge, <http://www.ntslibrary.com/PDF%20Books/Calvin%20Institutes%20of%20Christian%20Religion.pdf> [accessed 11 April 2015].

[95] The Westminster Assembly, *The Westminster Shorter Catechism with Proof Texts,* ed. by Robert B. Balsinger (CreateSpace Independent Publishing Platform [1647] 2010), p. 75.

[96] Acts 8.32–35.

[97] Col. 1.21–22.

[98] Heb. 9.24.

For such salvation to be brought about, Jesus ordained two sacraments; i.e. Baptism and the Supper of the Lord,[99] [100] which continue to be the fundamental sacramental roles of the modern-day priest within the Orthodox and Catholic traditions. Whilst acknowledging the controversy surrounding the question as to whether Jesus instituted the three orders of ministry (bishop, priest and deacon),[101] the point here is that Jesus exercised a ministry that combined both a priestly and a healing (physician-like) role; the priestly role being recognised both within the scriptures and also in Christianity's subsequent interpretation of the role of a priest.

The Significance of St Luke

Whilst recognising the suggestion that the term 'Christianity' was not used to describe the beliefs subscribed to by the followers of Jesus Christ until about 100 AD, the term 'Christian' was in use much earlier,[102] and any account of the connection between early Christianity as a movement and the medical profession would be inadequate without consideration

---

99 Catechism of *The Book of Common Prayer*.
100 Church of England, *The Book of Common Prayer* (Oxford: Oxford University Press, [1662] 1969), p. 350.
101 John Bowden, 'Ministry and Ministers: Origins of the ordained ministry' in: *Christianity: The Complete Guide,* ed. by John Bowden (London: Continuum, 2005), pp. 749–57.
102 The term 'Christians' to describe the disciples of Jesus was used *circa* 44 AD, and is referred to in Acts 11.26, whereas the term 'Christianity' is thought to have been derived by Ignatius of Antioch around 100 AD.

as to the role of the person who can be described as the 'first Christian physician'. That person is known as St Luke; an evangelist and writer who is believed to be the author[103] of the gospel according to St Luke[104] and the book of the Acts of the Apostles.[105]

That said, very little of substance is known about Luke's early life.[106] Nonetheless, there is little question about his place as an historian and theologian within the New Testament.[107] Indeed, his writings have been described as 'the storm centre of modern New Testament Study',[108] for such is their importance in trying to understand the life of Jesus, the work of his apostles, and the evolution of the early Christian Church.[109] However, specifically in respect to this dissertation, the aspect that has the greater pertinence is that Luke is understood to have been a physician.[110]

As with much of Luke's life, the evidence for him having been a physician is sparse, but nevertheless persuasive. In the Letter of Paul to the Colossians,

---

103 Adolf von Harnack and William Douglas Morrison, *Luke the Physician: the Author of the Third Gospel and the Acts of ten Apostles* (London: Williams and Norgate, 1908), pp. 121–45.
104 C. F. Evans, *Saint Luke* (London: SCM Press, 1990), p. 1.
105 Ibid., p. 4.
106 Eliza Allen Starr, *Patron Saints* (Montana: Kessinger Publishing, [1883] 2003), p. 322.
107 I. Howard Marshall, *Luke – Historian and Theologian*, 3rd edn (Carlisle: Paternoster, [1970] 1988), p. 18.
108 W. C. van Unnik, 'Luke-Acts, A Storm Center in Contemporary Scholarship', in: *Studies in Luke-Acts*, ed. by L. E. Keck and J. L. Martyn (Nashville: Abingdon, 1966), pp. 15–32.
109 Mark Powell, *What Are They Saying About Luke?* (New York: Paulist Press, 1989), p. 6.
110 Starr, p. 324.

The Christian Perspective

Paul refers to Luke as 'Luke, the beloved physician'.[111] An analysis by Hobart of Luke's writing, and the terms used therein, gave added substance to this viewpoint, with Hobart concluding that Luke's language was very much that of a medical doctor,[112] a view reinforced by many other 20th century scholars,[113] though not by all.[114] Others drew attention to the reference in Acts[115] in respect to 'healers who were showered with honors [sic] on the island of Melite',[116] stating that there is a strong argument for Luke having been amongst their number. The same scholars also referred to Luke's comment regarding the concept of 'physician, heal thyself',[117] with the suggestion that Luke is saying this in terms of the thoughts of others being reflected back at him in his capacity as a physician.[118]

In addition to the concept of Luke as 'historian, theologian and physician', Strelan has suggested that he might also have been a Jewish priest, thereby giving Luke the authority to write and interpret the life and work of Jesus as he has done.[119] If this were truly to be the case

---

111 Col. 4.14.
112 William Kirk Hobart, *The Medical Language of St Luke: A Proof from Internal Evidence that 'The Gospel According to St Luke' and 'The Acts of the Apostles' Were Written by the Same Person, and that the Writer was a Medical Man* (Dublin: Hodges, Figgis & Co., 1882).
113 Rick Strelan, *Luke the Priest: The Authority of the Author of the Third Gospel* (Aldershot: Ashgate, 2008), p.101.
114 Henry J. Cadbury, *The Style and Literary Method of Luke* (Cambridge: Harvard University Press, 1920), p. vi.
115 Acts 28.10.
116 Strelan, p. 101.
117 Lk. 4.23.
118 Strelan, p. 101.
119 Ibid., p. 1.

(some writers certainly disagree),[120] and recognising the fact that Christianity in the early 1st century was a subsect of the Jewish religion rather than an established and recognised religion in its own right, then it could also be argued that Luke was not only the first Christian physician, but just possibly the first Christian physician-priest. (A parochial twist to this links St Luke and a modern-day physician and potential ordinand – *vide infra*.)[121] [122] [123] [124]

The Church of England

Whilst it is not intended that this section should be comprehensive, there are a few disparate aspects relating to the Church of England that are related to the concept of the role of the physician-priest and are therefore considered to be worth commenting upon.

The first issue relates to the historic involvement of

---

120 John Wenham, 'The Identification of Luke', *The Evangelical Quarterly*, 63, no. 1 (1991), 3–44.
121 This relates to the examination of the purported remains of St Luke, and the extraction of mitochondrial DNA from a tooth in 1998. In 2011, this dissertation's author submitted his DNA to Cambridge University. The surprising result indicates a shared maternal motherline as those remains; thus providing (allowing for historic uncertainties) a genetic link between St Luke and this author; an intriguing 1st and 21st century connection between two 'physician-theologians' if not both 'physician-priests'!
122 Nicholas Wade, 'Body of St Luke Gains Credibility', *New York Times*, 16th October, 2001, <http://www.nytimes.com/2001/10/16/world/body-of-st-luke-gains-credibility.html> [accessed 19 April 2015].
123 Cristiano Vernesi and others, 'Genetic characterization of the body attributed to the evangelist Luke', *Proceedings of the National Academy of Sciences of the USA*, 98 (2001), pp. 13460–3.
124 Peter Foster (Geneticist), Cambridge, personal correspondence, December 2011.

the Church in respect to the awarding of medical degrees. As has been stated elsewhere,[125] under the Peter's Pence Act of 1533:[126]

> ...the Archbishop of Canterbury had the right to issue licences to practitioners within the Province of Canterbury (extending from 'England south of the Humber and the whole of Wales').[127]

The Lambeth Palace Library holds the *Directory of Medical Licences 1535-1775*, and this indicates that this right was frequently exercised by the Archbishop of Canterbury until the last dispensation issued in 1775.[128] Whilst these licences did not especially relate to ordained persons who were also practising medicine, their provision does serve to illustrate the close, direct involvement of the Church of England with the medical profession as far back as the early 16th century and that this continued into the late 18th century.

The second issue relates to the liturgy of the Church of England. Neither the Church of England nor the Roman Catholic Church has a specific 'Doctrine of Healing'; notwithstanding the interpretation of Christ's

---

125 Jaggs-Fowler, p. 36.
126 Otherwise known as the Ecclesiastical Licences Act 1533, the Act outlawed Peter's Pence (a payment previously made by landowners to the Pope) and transferred to Canterbury the right to issue dispensations previously issued by the Pope.
127 Lambeth Palace Library, *Lambeth Palace Library Research Guide: Medical Licences Issued by the Archbishop of Canterbury 1535-1775*, p. 2. <www.lambethpalacelibrary.org/files/Medical_Licences.pdf> [accessed 26 April 2015].
128 Lambeth Palace Library, op. cit.: 3.

atonement and the doctrine of salvation[129] in the catechism of the Catholic Church,[130] [131] or the inclusion of the matter of salvation within the Thirty Nine Articles of 1563,[132] which form part of the doctrine of the Church of England.[133] It is the modern-day Pentecostal Church that specifically refers to the Doctrine of Healing within the Atonement;[134] although it is true to say that this is more about spiritual healing rather than physical healing or the resolution of mental health issues.

The *Book of Common Prayer* continues to be the ultimate standard for all liturgical services within the Church of England,[135] as determined by Canons A3,[136] B1[137] and B3.[138] Within the Ordinal for the Ordination of Deacons, the liturgy states that, in respect to the ordinand:

And furthermore, it is his Office [...] to search for the sick [...] of the Parish [...].[139]

---

129 Alister E. McGrath, *Christian Theology*, p. 315.
130 The Holy See, *Catechism of the Catholic Church*, 2nd edn (Citta del Vaticano: Libreria Editrice Vaticana, 2000), 1565.
131 Ibid., p. 1992.
132 E. J. Bicknell, *A Theological Introduction to the Thirty-Nine Articles of the Church of England*, 3rd edn (Eugene: Wipf & Stock Publishers, 2007).
133 The Archbishops' Council, *The Canons of the Church of England*, 7th edn (London: Church House Publishing, 2012), A5, p. 7.
134 Living Faith Forum, *The Pentecostal Doctrine of Healing*, New Beginning Christian Ministries, <http://livingfaithforum.org/healing.html> [accessed 02 May 2015].
135 Davie, p. 154.
136 The Archbishops' Council, *The Canons of the Church of England*, p. 5.
137 Ibid., p. 13.
138 Ibid., pp. 17–18.
139 Church of England, 'The Ordering of Deacons', *The Book of Common Prayer*, p. 645.

The contemporary order of service for the ordination of deacons continues to reflect the above, reinforcing and exemplifying the same with the task to 'minister to the sick'.[140] It is therefore suggested that this again illustrates the fundamental healing mission of Christianity, and the close connection between the work of the priest and that of the physician.

In addition, in accordance with the scriptures wherein it is recorded that Jesus sent his disciples out 'to cure every disease and every sickness',[141] the Church of England does recognise the need for a healing ministry in respect to the sick,[142] and has a recognised liturgy for such ministry.[143] Indeed, a review of the ministry of healing was undertaken by the House of Bishops in 1998,[144] recognising that 'healing [...] is what the Church's mission is all about'.[145] The guidelines for such a ministry 'reflect the guidelines and codes of conduct and ethics [...] established for the medical [...] profession'.[146]

Finally, there is the issue of the nature of the Christian priesthood itself. This will be dealt with in detail within

---

140 The Archbishops' Council, *Common Worship: Services and Prayers for the Church of England: Ordination Services* (London: Church House Publishing, 2007), p. 15.
141 Mt. 10.1.
142 The Archbishops' Council, *A Time to Heal: The Development of Good Practice in the Healing Ministry: A Handbook* (London: Church House Publishing, 2000), p. 22.
143 The Archbishops' Council, *Common Worship: Services and Prayers for the Church of England: Ministry to the Sick* (London: Church House Publishing, 2000).
144 The Archbishops' Council, *A Time to Heal*, p. 1.
145 Ibid.
146 Ibid., p. 18.

the next chapter. However, it is worth reflecting here on part of the wording of the Church of England's Canon C24, which carries the title 'Of priests having a cure of souls'. The subsequent paragraphs of the canon lay down the obligations of a priest 'having a cure of souls' and includes the obligation to visit those who are in ill-health or frail.[147]

The 'cure of souls' (*cura animarum*) is an ancient ministry,[148] being referred to in the writings of both Christian[149] and Jewish[150][151] medieval theologians. It relates to the nurturing of that which 'describes the essence of each person';[152] 'the unfathomable depth of psyche',[153] and the human journey of spiritual 'healing and wholeness'. This in turn overlaps with the medical concept of physical 'health and well-being'. Indeed, it can be argued that the latter state cannot be achieved unless the former is also

---

147 The Archbishops' Council, *The Canons of the Church of England*, C 24 (6), p. 111.
148 Sue Pickering, *Spiritual Direction: A Practical Introduction* (Norwich: Canterbury Press, 2008), p. 7.
149 Robert Grosseteste, *Templum Dei* (c.1219-1225), ed. by Joseph Goering and F.A.C. Mantello (Toronto: Pontifical Institute of Medieval Studies, 1984).
150 Maimonides, *The Guide of the Perplexed*, Chaim Rabin (trans.), (Indianapolis: Hackett Publishing Company, 1952).
151 David Bakan, Dan Merkur and David S. Weiss, *Maimonides' Cure of Souls: Medieval Precursor of Psychoanalysis* (New York: State University of New York Press, 2009).
152 Andrew Powell and Christopher MacKenna, 'Psychotherapy', in: *Spirituality and Psychiatry*, ed. by Chris Cook, Andrew Powell and Christopher MacKenna (London: RCPsych Publications, 2009), pp. 101–21.
153 Michael Kearney and Radhule Weininger, 'Care of the soul', in: *Oxford Textbook of Spirituality in Healthcare*, ed. by Mark Cobb, Christina M. Puchalski and Bruce Rumbold (Oxford: Oxford University Press, 2012), pp. 273–8.

The Christian Perspective

addressed;[154] a holistic concept subscribed to in principle by Western medical authorities, including the General Medical Council, which, within its publication *Good Medical Practice* (wherein the expected standards of a medical doctor are laid down), quite clearly states the obligation to take a spiritual history.[155]

This recognition is reflected within the World Health Organisation's definition of health, which states that health is 'a state of complete physical, mental and social well-being, not merely the absence of disease or infirmity'.[156]

However, experience demonstrates that what is authoritatively promulgated within the medical profession in theory is not always officially supported in practice (*vide infra*). Nonetheless, from a Church of England perspective, the concept is firmly there and is carried through, not only in respect to the obligations of a parish priest, but also in relation to the work of spiritual directors,[157] with the skill set required of the spiritual director and pastoral counsellor significantly overlapping that of the medical counsellor or psychotherapist; which includes, amongst other things, the ability to establish a bond or affinity, facilitating the will to be open and candid, listening with an attentive ear, asking pertinent

---

154 David Greaves, *The Healing Tradition: Reviving the soul of Western medicine* (Oxford: Radcliffe Publishing, 2004), p. 17–18.
155 General Medical Council, *Good Medical Practice* (London: General Medical Council, 2013), p. 7.
156 World Health Organisation, *Constitution of the World Health Organisation* (New York: World Health Organisation, 1946), p. 1, < http://apps.who.int/gb/bd/PDF/bd47/EN/constitution-en.pdf> [accessed 28 April 2015].
157 Sue Pickering, p. 16.

questions, summarising topics discussed and emotions experienced.[158]

Indeed, to illustrate the intersecting holism further, the role of the spiritual director has even been somewhat gracefully described as a 'physician of souls';[159] an idea that chimes with Grosseteste's concept of the priest as 'a kind of medical assistant, administering spiritual medicine on behalf of the physician'.[160] [161] Furthermore, this discussion turns full circle when it is considered that, on many occasions, Jesus himself acted as a spiritual director as well as a priest and physician. Scriptural examples of his ministry in this respect include his discussion with Nicodemus,[162] that with two disciples on the way to Emmaus,[163] and his advice to the rich man.[164]

Summary

In this chapter, the activities of Jesus have been assessed and evidence produced to show how he fulfilled several functional roles, including those of being a priest, a healer (to some writers a healer being synonymous with a physician), and a spiritual director. A brief overview has also been given in respect to what is known about

---

158 Ibid.
159 Peter Ball, *Anglican Spiritual Direction* (Harrisburg: Morehouse Publishing, 2007), p. 14.
160 Peter Loewen, *Music in Early Franciscan Thought* (Leiden: Koninklijke Brill, 2013), p. 124.
161 Robert Grosseteste, *Templum Dei*, V1.4.
162 Jn 3.1–21.
163 Lk. 24.13–32.
164 Mk 10.17–22.

the background to St Luke, specifically in so much as the strong suggestion that he was a trained physician, and how he may have combined his work as a physician with that of being a theologian, possibly a priest, and also with writing a significant contribution of the gospels. These two examples of Jesus and such a major evangelist as Luke assist in consolidating the concept that, in practice as well as in theory, Christianity is a religion of healing and that the practical mix of healing and theology is at the very heart of the origins of Christianity.

The final part of this chapter looked at how the Anglican church was directly involved with the appointment of physicians during the 16th–18th centuries, and how the modern-day Church of England continues to place a particular emphasis on matters of caring for and, where possible, healing the sick and infirm, in the duties expected of its ordained ministers, from the practical role of the deacons in visiting the sick, to priests being entrusted with the cure of souls.

The fact that the two roles of priest and physician are so overlapping from the very birth of Christianity, through a period of two millennia, and still more than alluded to within the modern-day ordinal, paves the way for the considerations within the next chapter, those being:

☦ what are the individual roles of priests and physicians in the 21st century?
☦ how does society perceive those roles?
☦ can (and should) the two roles be comfortably and usefully combined within the form of one person?

III

Modern-Day Perspectives

This is the distinction: a doctor's door should never be closed, a priest's door should always be open.[165]

Victor Hugo (1802–1885)

The late 20th and early 21st centuries have seen a remarkable change in the attitude towards the interaction of religion and medicine. Despite the historical division of the two professions (*vide supra*), and in direct contrast to the common view that the Western world in the 21st century consists of secular societies,[166] [167] the number of university departments and centres for the study of the inter-relationship of spirituality, theology and health has been steadily increasing.[168] [169] In addition, papers

---

165 Victor Hugo, *Les Misérables* (London: Penguin Classics, [1862] 1982), p. 39.
166 Nick Cohen, 'Secular Britain is ruled by religious bureaucrats', *Guardian*, 16 December 2012 <http://www.theguardian.com/commentisfree/2012/dec/16/secular-britain-ruled-by-religious-bureaucrats> [accessed 25 May 2015].
167 Charles Taylor, *A Secular Age* (Cambridge, MA: Harvard University Press, 2007), p. 1.
168 Harold G. Koenig, Dana E. King and Verna Benner Carson, *Handbook of Religion and Health* 2nd edn (Oxford: Oxford University Press, 2012), p. 32.
169 For example, the Project for Spirituality, Theology and Health at Durham University, <https://www.dur.ac.uk/school.health/pg/taught/sth/> [accessed 15 March 2015].

reporting studies on the same are more frequently published in medical and scientific journals, and medical schools in the United Kingdom and United States of America are increasingly offering courses on the subject of 'Spirituality, Theology and Medicine'.[170] This is in some ways reflective of an evolving scholarly argument that the western world is now entering a 'post-secular'[171] phase of societal development that 'needs to adjust to the enduring presence of religion'.[172] As Micklethwait and Wooldridge stated in their popular analysis of the dynamism of religion in the 21st century, religion can be seen making a renaissance within public life, regardless as to whether one considers areas such as well-heeled states of the USA, slums of South American towns, or the suburbs of northern English cities.[173] That said, the latter is not a view that is, as yet, widely held within the popular press.[174] Nonetheless, the change in attitude by some aspects of the modern medical profession, in terms of recognising the need to consider spiritual and religious aspects of a patient's needs, has been recognised by the Church.[175] However, it is true to say that such co-

---

170 Koenig, pp. 33–34.
171 Wouter de Been and Sanne Taekema, 'Religion in the 21st Century: Debating the Post-Secular Turn', *Erasmus Law Review*, 5, no. 1 (2012), 1–3.
172 Ibid.
173 John Micklethwait and Adrian Wooldridge, *God is Back: How The Global Rise of Faith is Changing the World* (London: Penguin Books, 2009), p. 12.
174 John Bingham, 'Christianity now written off as fixation with "sky pixie" – Michael Gove', *Telegraph*, 01 April 2015, < http://www.telegraph.co.uk/news/religion/11510368/Christianity-now-written-off-as-fixation-with-sky-pixie-Michael-Gove.html> [accessed 23 May 2015].
175 The Archbishops' Council, *A Time to Heal*, p. 22.

operation is not exactly new, and was certainly a matter of discussion between the British Medical Association and the Church in 1956.[176]

The above reflects the advice now issued by the General Medical Council, which now states that the provision of good medical practice and care includes taking a spiritual history,[177] albeit with the later admonition to doctors that a doctor's personal beliefs should not form part of the conversation, patients should not be made distressed by the conversation, and exploitation of a patient's vulnerability should most certainly be avoided.[178] It is thus the case that physicians continue to tread uneasy ground in respect to the interface of medical practice and religious matters, as many have found to their personal cost.[179] [180]

The two medical specialities that are most likely to find the needs of patients overlapping the realms of medicine and religion are those of general practice and psychiatry, by virtue of their case mix. However, before considering further the possibility of formally recognising the physician-priest as a specific entity within the 21st century, it would be useful to tease out the specific individual characteristics and roles pertinent

---

176 British Medical Association, *Divine Healing and Co-operation Between Doctors and Clergy* (London: British Medical Association, 1956).
177 General Medical Council, *Good Medical Practice* (London: General Medical Council, 2013), p. 7.
178 Ibid., p. 18.
179 Clare Dyer, 'GP is struck off for imposing his religious views on a vulnerable patient', *BMJ*, 350 (2015), p. 4.
180 BBC, 'Faith row Margate GP Richard Scott gets formal warning', *BBC News Kent*, 14 June 2012, < http://www.bbc.co.uk/news/uk-england-kent-18445924> [accessed 23 May 2015].

to these professionals. In other words, to answer the questions as to what is meant by the term 'priest', and what is the specific role of a 'GP' or 'psychiatrist'?

The Role of the Priest

The dictionary's definition of 'priest' is a reasonable starting point, but lacks a certain clarity of function, referring as it does to ordained ministers who have authorisation to carry out specified services or rituals.[181] That may well be out of necessity for, as Carr points out, there is controversy over terms such as 'priest' and 'priesthood'.[182]

Williams provides some degree of clarity by referring to the *role* of the priest as outlined within the Old Testament, stating that such a person forms an understanding of both God and humanity and then explains one to the other, providing a link or pathway connecting one to the other, and thereby re-establishing broken affiliations.[183] A much longer description of the role of a priest is provided in the service for the ordination of priests,[184] wherein it states that priests are to:

☦ *be servants and shepherds*
☦ *proclaim the word of the Lord*
☦ *watch for the signs of God's new creation*

---

[181] Catherine Soanes (ed.), *Compact Oxford English Dictionary*, 2nd edn. (Oxford: Oxford University Press, 2000).
[182] Wesley Carr, *The Priestlike Task* (London: SPCK, 1985), p. 2.
[183] Rowan Williams, *Being Christian* (London: SPCK, 2014), p. 14.
[184] The Archbishops' Council, *Common Worship: Ordination Services*, p. 37.

- ✝ *be messengers, watchmen and stewards of the Lord*
- ✝ *teach and to admonish*
- ✝ *feed and provide for his family*
- ✝ *search for his children in the wilderness of this world's temptations*
- ✝ *guide them through its confusions*
- ✝ *call their hearers to repentance*
- ✝ *declare in Christ's name the absolution and forgiveness of their sins*
- ✝ *tell the story of God's love*
- ✝ *baptize new disciples in the name of the Father, and of the Son, and of the Holy Spirit*
- ✝ *walk with them in the way of Christ, nurturing them in the faith*
- ✝ *unfold the Scriptures*
- ✝ *preach the word in season and out of season*
- ✝ *declare the mighty acts of God*
- ✝ *preside at the Lord's table*
- ✝ *lead his people in worship*
- ✝ *bless the people in God's name*
- ✝ *resist evil*
- ✝ *support the weak*
- ✝ *defend the poor*
- ✝ *intercede for all in need*
- ✝ *minister to the sick*
- ✝ *prepare the dying for their death*
- ✝ *discern and foster the gifts of all God's people.*

The complexity of the aforementioned role description lends credence to the concept that 'there is no one way of being a priest'.[185] Indeed, it is pertinent to be reminded that 'there is only one Christian priesthood, and that is the priesthood of Christ'.[186] The term 'presbyter' may therefore be a less controversial term to describe the office of 'priest'; a presbyter being more simply defined as 'an elder or minister of the Christian Church';[187] the latter being in keeping with the perspective that it is not possible to be ordained in the abstract – ordination can only be in relation to a specific community and, of itself, invokes the requisite of service to that community.[188]

Furthermore, Peter tells us that the elders (presbyters) of the community have an obligation to God to lead others in the way of faith.[189] Indeed, Peter insists on recognising 'the priestly character and ministry of God's people',[190] thus suggesting that presbyters may be called *priests* only because they allow the people in turn to be *priestly*,[191] as is the scripturally-based task of all Christians.[192]

Such is the difficulty in defining a priest that the House of Bishops sought to lend clarity to the issue in 1997,[193] stating that a priest is *de facto* the embodiment of

---

185 Rowan Williams, *A Ray of Darkness* (Cambridge MA: Cowley, 1995), p. 157.
186 Christopher Cocksworth and Rosalind Brown, *Being A Priest Today*, 2nd edn (Norwich: Canterbury Press, [2002] 2006), p. 9.
187 Catherine Soanes (ed.), *Compact Oxford English Dictionary*.
188 Cocksworth and Brown, p. 17.
189 1 Pet. 5.1-2.
190 Cocksworth and Brown, p. 9.
191 Ibid., p. 26.
192 Eph. 4.1-13.
193 House of Bishops of the General Synod, *Eucharistic Presidency: A Theological Statement* (London: Church House Publishing, 1997).

the Four Marks of the Church (those being: oneness, holiness, catholicity and apostolicity).[194]

The Role of the Physician

At face value, the role of the 'physician' might appear to be easier to define than that of the 'priest'. The OED is quite clear on the matter, dogmatically stating that a physician is 'a person qualified to practise medicine'; with an identical definition being given to the term 'doctor'. The same source simply states that a 'general practitioner' is 'a community doctor'. The difficulty starts to arise when clarification is sought in respect to the term 'medicine', which is given as 'the science or practice of the treatment and prevention of disease', with 'disease' being defined as 'a disorder of structure or function'. Gradually, as the various terms are unpicked, the definitions become increasingly veiled in etymological obfuscation.

From a medical perspective, the Leeuwenhorst definition of general practice is frequently used:

The general practitioner is a licensed medical graduate who gives personal, primary and continuing care to individuals, families and a practice population irrespective of age, sex and illness. It is the synthesis of these functions which is unique.[195]

---

194 Cocksworth and Brown, p. 24.
195 *Vocational training in general practice,* ed. by J. Heyrman and C. Spreeuwenbergh (Leuven: Katholieke Universiteit Leuven, 1987).

However, this is considered by some to be outdated,[196] and certainly doesn't contain the quality and core values as laid down by the GMC,[197] nor the exhortation that GPs will:

> ...*be aware of and take account of physical, psychological and social factors in looking after their patients.*[198]

Psychiatrists, the second of the medical specialists that most frequently need to consider the spiritual and religious needs of patients on a routine basis, fare little better in terms of being defined. The NHS simply states that 'psychiatrists deal with mental health'.[199] The American Psychiatric Association is a little more expansive, defining a psychiatrist as 'a physician who specializes in the diagnosis, treatment, and prevention of mental health and emotional problems'; all of which begs the question as to the meaning of the term 'mental health'. The latter is again not an easy concept to pin down, being variously described as 'an absence of mental disorder',[200] or to that which 'includes our emotional, psychological, and social well-being',[201] or the very long-winded and complex

---

196 Frede Olesen, Jim Dickinson and Per Hjortdahl, 'General practice—time for a new definition', *BMJ* (2000) 320, pp. 354–7.
197 General Medical Council, *Good Medical Practice*.
198 NHS, *NHS Careers: General Practice*, <http://www.nhscareers.nhs.uk/explore-by-career/doctors/careers-in-medicine/general-practice/> [accessed 3 June 2015].
199 NHS, *NHS Careers: Psychiatry*, <http://www.nhscareers.nhs.uk/explore-by-career/doctors/careers-in-medicine/psychiatry/> [accessed 3 June 2015].
200 About Health, *What is Mental Health?*, <http://mentalhealth.about.com/cs/stressmanagement/a/whatismental.htm> [accessed 04 June 2015].
201 MentalHealth.gov, *What is Mental Health?*, <http://www.mentalhealth.gov/basics/what-is-mental-health/> [accessed 04 June 2015].

description within the 2001 World Health Organisation report, which concludes that 'it is nearly impossible to define mental health comprehensively'.[202]

Despite, or because of, the difficulties in defining these various roles and terms, what becomes abundantly clear is that, whether a GP or a psychiatrist, the physician's role is very close to that of the priest; which should not be entirely unexpected when the term 'doctor' is from the Latin for 'teacher',[203] and the word 'psychiatry' stems from the Greek for 'soul or mind' and 'healing'.[204] When compared with the priest's 'cure of souls' (*vide supra*), it is perhaps not surprising that a Cuban once remarked that 'the family doctor should be the new priest of the Revolution'.[205]

The Physician-Priest

As has been stated above and recognised as far back as the 6th century by Gregory the Great,[206] the work of the Christian physician and priest often overlaps; something that was reiterated in more recent times.[207] However, this acknowledgement in 1956 did not come without a warning:

---

202 World Health Organisation, *The World Health Report 2001: Mental Health – New Understanding, New Hope* (Geneva: WHO, 2001), p. 5.
203 'Doctor' is an agentive noun of the verb *docēre*, 'to teach'.
204 From *psukhē* (soul, mind) plus *iatreia* (healing).
205 Johanna Shapiro, 'Knowing What a Human Life Really Is: Doctors and Priests', *Family Medicine* 32, 9 (2000), 598–99.
206 H. R. Bramley (trans.), Gregory the Great, *On the Pastoral Charge* (Oxford: James Parker, 1874), p. 129.
207 British Medical Association, *Divine Healing and Co-operation Between Doctors and Clergy*, p. 24.

Neither clergyman nor doctor [...] should trespass into the field of the other, but where their work, which is essentially for individual people, overlaps they can easily co-operate.[208]

Nonetheless, as the 19th century writer Jean-Baptiste Alphonse Karr stated: 'plus ça change, plus c'est la même chose';[209] for, in 2011, an independent commission reporting on medical generalism wrote:

In some ways [...] the generalist can be seen as fulfilling for many people the type of role that a local priest would have occupied for them in former years: a respected figure who could be turned to for non-judgemental advice on a range of issues including, but not limited to, health care.[210]

It was a view that subsequently found echoes in the popular press, such as a reflection by Parris, writing in The Times in 2012, wherein he likened the current work of family doctors to that which was historically performed by parish priests; his view being supported by the concept that many of the problems seen by family doctors are as a result of psychological unrest rather than physical illness.[211]

---

208 Ibid.
209 Jean-Baptiste Alphonse Karr, *Les Guêpes*, vol. vi. (Paris: Société Belge de librairie, Jan 1849).
210 Ilora Finlay of Llandaff (Chair), *Guiding Patients Through Complexity: Modern Medical Generalism*, (London: The Royal College of General Practitioners and The Health Foundation, 2011), p. 8. <http://www.health.org.uk/public/cms/75/76/4299/2763/COMMISSION%20REPORT%20ON%20MEDICAL%20GENERALISM%20OCTOBER%202011.pdf?realName=xbuUe5.pdf> [accessed 24 May 2015].
211 Matthew Parris, 'GPs will soothe you, but won't really cure you', *The Times*, 15th September 2012, < http://www.thetimes.co.uk/tto/opinion/

In some eyes, this is certainly the case in respect to psychiatrists,[212] where the subject of guilt is frequently found to be a common denominator within those seeking assistance from priests and psychiatrists.[213] Indeed, in this respect, the psychiatrist's couch has been likened to the priest's confessional.[214]

From the GP's perspective, patients often attend with 'maladies of lifestyle'[215] and social problems. The suggestion has been made that this is because GPs are the only unbiased people patients can think of approaching when life takes a turn for the worse,[216] which in turn perhaps reflects our society's tendency towards a 'heresy of aloofness, a humanist belief in human difference'[217] to the point where the priest *per se* no longer has a recognised relevance for the major part of the population. This reality (for some) was emphasised by a particular patient's response when asked 'what is the doctor's job?' The patient responded 'for me, the doctor is now God [...] Now, there is only the doctor to protect me from the things around us'.[218]

That said, there sits an interesting contradiction

---

columnists/matthewparris/article3538931.ece> [accessed 25 May 2015].
212 A. C. P. Sims, 'The Psychiatrist as Priest', *Journal of the Royal Society of Health*, 5 (1988), 160–3.
213 Ibid.
214 Ibid.
215 Jim Pink, Lionel Jacobson and Mike Pritchard, 'The 21st century GP: physician and priest?' *British Journal of General Practice*, 57, 543 (2007), 840–3.
216 Ibid.
217 Robert Macfarlane, *The Wild Places* (London: Granta Books, 2007), p. 203.
218 Eric J. Cassell, *The Healer's Art: A New Approach to the Doctor-Patient Relationship* (Harmondsworth: Penguin, 1978), pp. 151–2.

when account is taken of the 2011 census data, wherein approximately 59.3% of the population of England and Wales identified themselves as Christian[219] (rising to 66.6% in the author's rural community in North Lincolnshire),[220] and thus it may have something more to do with the fact that the majority of people have lost regular communication with their parish priest[221] [222] and see the GP as being able to fulfil the same role in respect to assisting with their non-physical needs (such as bereavement counselling, the instillation of hope into moments of suffering and despair, the softening of guilt in respect to various 'sins', such as adultery, drug use, theft and fighting, and quite often the simple need to have someone to talk to in order to combat loneliness and social isolation). It is doubtless true to say that 'the spiritual role that used to be in the domain of the priests is now thrust into the medical sphere'.[223]

So, the 21st century GP clearly has a pastoral role

---

219 Office for National Statistics, *Religious Affiliation, England and Wales, 2011*, <http://www.ons.gov.uk/ons/rel/census/2011-census/key-statistics-for-local-authorities-in-england-and-wales/sty-religion.html> [accessed 05 June 2015].
220 Office for National Statistics, *2011 Census*.
221 It is estimated that just over one million people attend a Church of England service once per week. See: Tim Wyatt, 'C of E attendance statistics slope still points downward', *Church Times*, 14 November 2014, <http://www.churchtimes.co.uk/articles/2014/14-november/news/uk/c-of-e-attendance-statistics-slope-still-points-downward> [accessed 05 June 2015].
222 Archbishops' Council, *Church Statistics 2010/11: Parochial attendance, membership and finance statistics together with statistics of licensed ministers for the Church of England, January to December* (London: Archbishops' Council Research and Statistics, Central Secretariat, 2012), 1.
223 Jim Pink et al., 'The 21st century GP: physician and priest?'

in addition to the purely medical one. This is concisely expressed in the abstract to a paper by Barnard (1985), which states:

> *Despite much resistance from the medical profession, the notion persists in our culture that the physician plays a priestly role. Medical resistance must be taken seriously. It stems from legitimate concerns that the priestly role implies an unwelcome broadening of medical responsibilities, expectations of moral expertise, and being on the receiving end of people's most intense existential hopes. On the other hand, the nature of illness and healing makes it inevitable that physicians will take on ministerial functions in their medical work.*[224]

Indeed, one of the most frequently heard phrases of acknowledgement from patients in the author's personal experience is 'thank you for listening'; thus, emphasising the expectation of empathy, care and compassion in addition to scientific medical knowledge. Osler even emphasised that, without faith, 'man can do nothing';[225] but with faith 'all things are possible to him'.[226] For some, the association between physician and priest is even greater, with both having (by virtue of their knowledge and relationship with life and death) an ingrained 'charismatic authority'.[227] It is for these reasons that the

---

224 David Barnard, 'The Physician as Priest, Revisited', *Journal of Religion and Health*, 24, 4 (1985), 272–86.
225 William Osler, 'Medicine in the Nineteenth Century', in: William Osler, *Aequanimita and Other Addresses* (London: H. K. Lewis, 1946), pp. 258–60.
226 Ibid.
227 James A. Knight, 'The Minister as Healer, the Healer as Minister', *Journal of Religion and Health*, 21, 2 (1982), 101.

stated concept of some professional bodies (both medical and religious), and lay writers, is that the two roles of priest and physician, once historically bound within the same person and then slowly evolving into two distinct professions, have significantly re-merged within the modern-day roles of the General Medical Practitioner (GP) and the psychiatrist.

In 2011, Cox wrote a paper called 'Doctors, Clergy and the troubled Soul: two professions, one vocation?'[228] It is this author's perception that the answer to that question is decidedly in the affirmative. Accepting that there is considerable evidence to support that stance, the question for the future is whether there is room for a 'one profession, one vocation' model in the form of the physician-priest. Some clinicians would certainly answer in the affirmative, and Scott has provided an interesting example of a clinical case whereby, during the course of treating his patient, he fulfilled, in his view, the role of a 'physician-priest':

...hypnosis and religious belief were effectively combined to rid a patient of a long-term, emotional turmoil, ineffectively treated by other modalities...[229]

---

228 John Cox, 'Doctors, Clergy and the troubled Soul: two professions, one vocation?' Royal College of Psychiatrists (2011), <http://www.gohealth.org.uk/Report%20on%20SPSIG%20meeting%202.11.11.%20Cox.pdf> [accessed 05 June 2015].

229 Edward M. Scott, 'Combining the Roles of "Priest" and "Physician": A Clinical Case', *Journal of Religion and Health*, 18, 2 (1979), 160-3.

Summary

In his poem 'Days',[230] Larkin pictured '...the priest and the doctor/In their long coats/Running over the fields'[231] to assist in the solving of the question 'what are days for?'[232] and, by inference, to aid in providing an answer to the question regarding the meaning of life itself. Larkin clearly saw the priest and the doctor as having complementary, if not overlapping, roles. With Larkin's self-confessed ambivalence towards religion, as witnessed in his letters[233] as well as his poetry,[234] he might just as easily have referred to the 'physician-priest in his long coat...'.

It has been suggested that Western medicine's narrow focus on a scientifically-based approach to healing, with little or no religious or spiritual input, is 'an aberration on the world scene'.[235] However, for most people, ill-health is more than just a biological or physical malfunction. In its severest manifestations, disease is, as has been aptly described, 'an existential crisis'[236] that requires more than the cold dispensing of scientifically-based advice, void of all moral and spiritual ingredients. The

---

230 Philip Larkin, *Collected Poems* (London and Boston: The Marvell Press and Faber and Faber, 1988), p. 67.
231 Ibid., lines 8–9.
232 Ibid., line 1.
233 John Shakespeare, 'Philip Larkin: An Extraordinary Series of Letters from Philip Larkin to John Shakespeare' (*The Telegraph*, 23 April 2009), <http://www.telegraph.co.uk/culture/books/bookreviews/5207870/Philip-Larkin.html> [accessed 06 June 2015].
234 See 'Church Going' in Philip Larkin, *Collected Poems*, p. 97.
235 David Barnard, 'The Physician as Priest, Revisited'.
236 Ibid.

process of healing is something that is not solely within the powers of the physician. Indeed, in some cases, the physician is rendered powerless if constrained to the use of evidence-based medicine and prevented in addressing more spiritual matters. In such circumstances, the priest has an overlapping role with the physician, and this can be particularly seen in the medical worlds of general practice and psychiatry, thus raising modern debate about the two professions sharing the same vocation, and thus harkening back to the historical priest-physicians.

IV

The Future Perspective

If the head and body are to be well, you must begin by curing the soul; that is the first thing.[237]

Plato

Thirty years ago, a challenge was made to the medical profession and the Church. The writer said, 'the question is not *whether* physicians should take on priestly roles, but rather *how?*'[238] He went on to suggest that 'the task ahead is an occasion for self-examination and recovery of roots within both professions'.[239]

That physician-priests existed in the 20th century, and still do in the 21st century, is a matter of extensive

---

[237] Benjamin Jowett (trans.), 'The Dialogues of Plato: Charmides, or Temperance' (380BC) 156d3 – 157c6, in: Mortimer J. Adler (ed.), *Great Books Vol. 6: Plato,* 2nd edn (Chicago: Encyclopaedia Britannica Inc., [1952] 1990), pp. 1–13.
[238] David Barnard, 'The Physician as Priest, Revisited'.
[239] Ibid.

The Future Perspective

record within the UK,[240][241][242][243] the USA[244][245][246][247][248] and other areas of the Christian World.[249][250][251] It is also not unknown for other health professionals, such

---

240 Laura Hammond, 'Doctor turned Vicar takes on new role at Burton churches', *Burton Mail*, 12 December 2014, <http://www.burtonmail.co.uk/Doctor-turned-vicar-takes-new-role-Burton/story-22800557-detail/story.html> [accessed 07 June 2015].
241 Colin Tourle, 'Peter Wallis: Anglican priest and former general practitioner', *BMJ*, 349 (2014), p. 25.
242 Lucy Ward, 'Una Kroll: "Public protest is still very important"', *Guardian*, 17 November 2014, <http://www.theguardian.com/lifeandstyle/2014/nov/17/una-kroll-nun-doctor-priest-women-interview> [accessed 07 June 2015].
243 Durham University, *Profiles: Professor Chris Cook*, <https://www.dur.ac.uk/theology.religion/staff/profile/?id=3700> [accessed 07 June 2015].
244 Robyn Sidersky, 'Doctor-turned-priest faces new challenge to overcome: learning to walk again', *The Patriot News*, 19 January 2011, http://www.pennlive.com/midstate/index.ssf/2011/01/doctor-turned-priest_faces_new.html> [accessed 07 June 2015].
245 Michael Winerip, 'When A Physician Becomes A Priest', *New York Times*, 29 May 1986, <http://articles.sun-sentinel.com/1986-05-29/features/8602010910_1_monk-new-priest-roman-catholic-priest> [accessed 07 June 2015].
246 Malea Hargett, 'Former Arkansan provides healing as a priest and doctor', *Arkansas Catholic*, 28 October 2006, <http://www.arkansas-catholic.org/news/article/675> [accessed 07 June 2015].
247 William Bole, 'Jesuit MDs: Walking with Ignatius on Their Medical Rounds', <http://www.sjnen.org/Document.Doc?id=39> [accessed 07 June 2015].
248 Editorial, 'Doctor-Turned-Priest Makes Villages in Southern India "Blood Literate"', *UCA-News.com*, 09 June 2004, <http://www.ucanews.com/story-archive/?post_name=/2004/06/09/doctorturnedpriest-makes-villages-in-southern-india-blood-literate&post_id=24280> [accessed 07 June 2015].
249 Rocco Palmo, 'Jesuit, Priest, Physician, "Rock Star"', *Whispers in the Loggia*, 16 August 2006, <http://whispersintheloggia.blogspot.co.uk/2006/08/jesuit-priest-physician-rock-star.html> [accessed 07 June 2015].
250 Editorial, 'Doctor's Visit Nets New Parish Priest', *The Church of the GOC of America*, 07 February 2013, < http://www.hotca.org/parishes/417-doctors-visit-nets-new-parish-priest> [accessed 07 June 2015].
251 Omar Gharzeddine, 'Italian Priest and Medical Doctor, American NGO, Win 2014 United Nations Population Award', *United Nations Population Fund*, 21 March 2014, <http://www.unfpa.org/news/italian-priest-and-medical-doctor-american-ngo-win-2014-united-nations-population-award> [accessed 07 June 2015].

as nurses, to be ordained as priest whilst continuing to work within the NHS,[252] and the author knows of at least one practising GP who is currently training as a Reader in the Church of England.[253] These professionals continue to pursue a vocation that is underpinned by the desire to bring about healing in its broadest sense.

However, within the modern medical profession, healing in the holistic sense is being undermined by the relentless drive for meeting financial and outcomes targets and utilising evidence-based therapies, to the point whereby the traditional general practitioner is arguably at risk of losing the charismatic authority that heretofore has been an essential vocational prerequisite. One way forward, for both the medical profession and the Church, is the emergence of an enhanced, combined, healing ministry, being clinically-led, but under the auspices of the Church; what some call a 'new medical cosmology'.[254]

The promotion of the study of 'medical humanities'[255] as part of undergraduate medical training has been an early and vital step in the right direction. However, for such enlightened teaching to change professional healthcare-system attitudes and influence existing post-qualification prejudices, there needs to be

---

252 For example, the Rev'd Julia Clark is an Assistant Priest at St Hugh's Church, Old Brumby, North Lincolnshire and a practice nurse, <https://www.facebook.com/pages/St-Hughs-Church-Old-Brumby/412046958915218?sk=timeline&ref=page_internal> [accessed 07 June 2015].
253 Dr Jenny Ballantyne, GP, North Thoresby, Lincolnshire (personal correspondence, 16 May 2015).
254 Greaves, p. 149.
255 Ibid., p. 125.

a fundamental, radical and pioneering transformation of thinking and behaviour. Such radical challenge to the normative cannot easily come from within the medical profession operating solely within the traditional healthcare system; the combined forces of the GMC and NHS, and possibly elements of the medical Royal Colleges, would almost inevitably result in strong and oppressive opposition, whether by intention or default. It is therefore this author's conviction that the future of a healing vocation lies with the rise and acceptance of dually qualified physician-priests. In that respect, the Church needs to be bold in 'stepping up to the plate' in recognising, supporting and training such individuals, as well as providing the platform for a new expression of supplementary health care within the 21st century. In essence, it is the use of medicine as a conduit for applied, or practical, theology; the latter being tradition, faith and reason intersected with modern experience, queries and concepts, in a two-way interchange that is of inspirational, rational and substantially formative value,[256] and results, quite literally, in the Church and Society being served in practical ways by the results of Christian reflection and perspectives.[257]

The seeds for such transformation are already there in the existence of the aforementioned physician-priests (albeit usually working as 'physicians' and 'priests' within

---

[256] Stephen Pattison and James Woodward, *A Vision of Pastoral Theology* (Edinburgh: Contact Pastoral, 1994), p. 9.
[257] Paul Ballard and John Pritchard, *Practical Theology in Action*, 2nd edn (London: SPCK, 2006).

different vocational departments of their lives, rather than fulfilling the combined roles contemporaneously), and also by virtue of the existing recognition by the Church of the importance of its own, theologically-rooted healing ministry. By necessity, the development of such 'seeds' is likely to be slow and iterative. Nonetheless, the mechanisms that might allow such germination are already in place and well-recognised.

The concept of part-time priests is not new. Discussions were taking place at least as far back as the 1960s regarding the possibility of non-stipendiary ministers (NSMs) supplementing parish ministries. Then thought of as 'revolutionary' in England,[258] NSMs currently constitute two-thirds of the 28,000 licensed ministers in the Church of England.[259] Now more commonly known as 'self-supporting ministry' (SSM),[260] many of these priests are also working within some form of other employment and are frequently referred to as 'Ministers in Secular Employment' (MSEs),[261] thereby effectively reversing the 'hang-over from the dualism of sacred and secular'.[262] This has important, positive implications for the concept of a more definitive role for

---

258 F.R. Barry, 'The Case for Part Time Priests', in: *Part Time Priests?,* ed. by Robin Denniston (London: Skeffington, 1960), p. 14.
259 Linda Woodhead, 'Not enough boots on the ground', *Church Times,* 07 February 2014, <http://www.churchtimes.co.uk/articles/2014/7-february/features/features/not-enough-boots-on-the-ground> [accessed 10 June 2015].
260 Davie, p. 114.
261 Paul Needle, CPAS Resource Sheet 9: *Ministers in Secular Employment,* <http://www.cpas.org.uk/download/1204/web_upload%252F9%2BSeculaRemployment%2BRS09-single-1268750864.pdf> [accessed 10 June 2015].
262 Barry, p. 14.

the physician-priest in the 21st century, for it is not only something 'indubitably apostolic and primitive'[263] but therein emphasises the fundamental foundation of the priestly function.

There is no doubt that many doctors who are also ordained find several ways to exercise their ministry. For many, it will be as assistant curates within their parish churches, at the same time utilising their Christian beliefs and standards quietly within the background of their secular employment. Others may function as spiritual directors, otherwise known as 'Companions on the Way'[264] or 'Soul Friends'.[265] However, fulfilling though these vocations must be, none fully utilise the gifts, skills and knowledge of the 'physician-priest'. It is here that the more recent models of ministry open the possibility of a new, ground-breaking relationship between the Church and health care. One such example is known as Fresh Expressions.

Fresh Expressions[266] is the Church of England's initiative to further the concept of Pioneer Ministry,[267] reaching out to those 'who are not yet members of any church'.[268] However, this does not necessarily mean

---

263 Michael Ramsay, *The Christian Priest Today* (London: SPCK, 1972), p. 1.
264 Diocese of Lincoln, *Spiritual Direction: Companions on the Way*, <http://www.lincoln.anglican.org/resources-parishes-ministry/spirituality/spiritual-direction/> [accessed 04 July 2015].
265 Pickering, p. 25.
266 Fresh Expressions, <https://www.freshexpressions.org.uk/> [accessed 12 June 2015].
267 The Church of England, *Pioneer Ministry*, < https://www.churchofengland.org/clergy-office-holders/ministry/selection/pioneer-ministry.aspx> [accessed 12 June 2015].
268 The Church of England, *Exploring Pioneer Ministry: A Short Guide*,

working in isolation (for that was not the intention of Jesus),[269] or to be separate from an existing parish community. Indeed, it could be an arm of an existing parish community, or even part of an entire deaconry, and in many ways represents the diaconal ministry at its best.

It is suggested that one area where such pioneering work could be of great benefit, if led by a physician-priest, is in respect to the elderly; many of whom are patients with dementia or several long-term conditions. For such patients, it is no longer a matter of trying to cure their disease, but one of healing their suffering.

At present, *healing* is something that modern healthcare does not necessarily embrace in a comprehensive, positive and determined manner. The technical advances of the 20th century have allowed doctors to experience far greater success than ever before in terms of curing disease, with the result that ideas of 'healing' have become anachronistic.[270]

Yet, as the Secretary of State for Health recently stated, it is anticipated that those living with three or more long-term conditions will rise by 50% to three million by 2018, and by 2020 there will be a million more people over the age of 70 and 100,000 more people needing care at home.[271] This is in addition to the problem of

---

p. 2. <https://www.freshexpressions.org.uk/sites/default/files/ExploringPioneerMinistry_2.pdf> [accessed 20 June 2015].
269 Lk. 10:1.
270 Cassell, p. 16.
271 Jeremy Hunt, *New Deal for General Practice* (London: Department of Health, 2015), <https://www.gov.uk/government/speeches/new-deal-for-general-practice> [accessed 20 June 2015].

The Future Perspective

dementia, which currently affects 676,000 in the UK;[272] a figure that is set to double by 2030.[273] It is an area of societal need that is set to exceed the current capacity of the healthcare services. However, the need for healing is immense within these groups, both in respect to those who are afflicted and those who act as their carers. The power to provide such healing is potentially in the hands of the Church; for, even with dementia, 'as long as God remembers us, who we are will remain'.[274]

In this respect, it could be claimed that it is the Church's responsibility to bring into the present God's promise to engrave our names on the palm of His hand.[275] That very commission may well be a role for the 21st century physician-priest and might be deemed to be a form of 'sector ministry'[276] in terms of its health-related specificity. Just how and where such a ministry might be exercised is open to discernment. Nonetheless, the home environment might be a very good starting point, therein reflecting the very direction given by Jesus to his disciples upon instructing them in respect to their healing ministry.[277]

In practical terms, the above concept opens a

---

272 Department of Health, *Prime Minister's challenge on dementia 2020* (London: Department of Health, 2015), p. 5.
273 Alzheimer's Disease International, *World Alzheimer's Report 2014: Dementia and Risk Reduction – an analysis of protective and modifiable factors* (London: Alzheimer's Disease International, 2014), <http://www.alz.co.uk/research/world-report-2014> [accessed 20 June 2015].
274 John Swinton, *Dementia: Living in the Memories of God* (Michigan: Eerdmans, 2012), 197.
275 Isa. 49:15–16.
276 Davie, p. 224.
277 Lk. 9.1–6.

significant range of possibilities for the Church in relation to its relationship with society as a whole, and with the NHS and Local Authorities in particular. This may be best expressed through a relationship with the Health and Wellbeing Boards,[278] which were established as statutory bodies in 2012.[279] Funding for healthcare work by teams led by physician-priests may be possible from the £3.8billion Better Care Fund;[280] the latter being designed to support integrated health and social care services.[281] Funding may also be possible under an APMS Contract,[282] which allows NHS commissioners to award contracts for healthcare services to non-NHS providers, such as voluntary or commercial sector providers,[283] thereby relieving some of the pressure on existing primary healthcare services.

As part of this model of care by the Church, it may be that some existing physician-priests may take a lead role, seeing it as an opportunity to truly combine their two inter-related vocations without incurring the wrath of

---

278 Department of Health, *A Short Guide to Health and Wellbeing Boards*, <http://webarchive.nationalarchives.gov.uk/20130805112926/http://healthandcare.dh.gov.uk/hwb-guide/> [accessed 20 June 2015].
279 Health and Social Care Act 2012.
280 NHS England, *Better Care Fund Planning*, <http://www.england.nhs.uk/ourwork/part-rel/transformation-fund/bcf-plan/> [accessed 20 June 2015].
281 Department of Health and Department for Communities and Local Government, *Better Care Fund 2015/2016: Policy Framework*, <https://www.gov.uk/government/uploads/system/uploads/attachment_data/file/381848/BCF.pdf> [20 June 2015].
282 NHS England, *NHS England Standard Alternative Provider Medical Services Contract 2014/2015*, <http://www.england.nhs.uk/wp-content/uploads/2014/06/apms-standard-contract-june14.pdf> [accessed 20 June 2015].
283 Ibid.

the GMC. Local teams may also be from the virtual bank of retired Christian doctors and nurses, many of whom are still keen to be involved in some part-time (possibly voluntary) way in serving their local communities, but do not wish to continue working purely within the conventional health setting.

However, it is suggested that there is an even greater visionary concept that would more firmly integrate the Church within the wider society; that is, if the Church considered ways in which it might sponsor the training of some doctors, whom it would also train as priests, thus producing purpose-made physician-priests. Such combined training is not without precedent in other walks of life. For example, the UK military sponsors people to train as doctors or nurses whilst also preparing them for a role within military life.[284]

With imagination and funding, it might even be possible to develop a 'theological-medical college', specifically geared to the training of physician-priests. Once again, comparators exist elsewhere. For example, the Bishop Grosseteste University[285] in Lincoln was initially established as an Anglican teacher training college, and now functions as a Church of England university. Alternatively, and as a further, albeit parochial, example of the possibilities, the existing Lincoln School

---

284 Army, *Funding Support: Medical Services bursary*, <http://www.army.mod.uk/training_education/25683.aspx> [accessed 20 June 2015].
285 Bishop Grosseteste University, <http://www.bishopg.ac.uk/Pages/default.aspx> [accessed 20 June 2015].

of Theology[286] might enter a partnership arrangement with an existing medical school, such as the Hull-York Medical School,[287] or act to co-develop a fresh style of medical school within the University of Lincoln.[288] Such inter-relationships already exist elsewhere within the Christian world. For example, at least four medical schools in the USA[289] [290] [291] [292] are run by the Jesuits,[293] and as of 2010, there were at least twenty-five Jesuit physicians in the USA who exercised a dual ministry.[294]

Summary

It has been stated that the affiliation between 'Church' and 'Society' is a rapidly moving concept and that, if churches are to remain relevant within their communities, it is necessary for them to seriously consider how to exercise that vocation within the contemporary context.[295]

---

286 Diocese of Lincoln, *Lincoln School of Theology*, <http://www.lincoln.anglican.org/education-training/lincoln-school-of-theology/> [accessed 20 June 2015].
287 Hull York Medical School, <http://www.hyms.ac.uk/> [accessed 20 June 2015].
288 University of Lincoln, <http://www.lincoln.ac.uk/home/> [accessed 20 June 2015].
289 Creighton University School of Medicine <http://medschool.creighton.edu/> [accessed 04 July 2015].
290 Georgetown University School of Medicine <https://som.georgetown.edu/> [accessed 04 July 2015].
291 Loyola University, Stritch School of Medicine <http://ssom.luc.edu/> [accessed 04 July 2015].
292 Saint Louis University School of Medicine <http://www.slu.edu/medicine> [accessed 04 July 2015].
293 The Jesuits, <http://jesuits.org/aboutus> [accessed 04 July 2015].
294 Bole, William, 'Jesuit MDs: Walking with Ignatius on Their Medical Rounds', *Jesuits*, 2010, 12–13.
295 Department of Theology, *Doctor of Theology and Ministry Handbook*

This chapter reflects that statement and has been a speculative examination as to how the future could look in respect to the development of physician-priests, with particular reference to the Church of England. Evidence has been presented to demonstrate that many healthcare professionals exercise the ministry of the priesthood alongside, though outwardly distinct from, their secular profession of physician or nurse. Examples have also been presented showing how a religious foundation (in this case the Jesuits) is active in the field of medical education in the USA, with the result that some Jesuits exercise the dual role of priest and physician as one ministry, seeking to care for their patients in their totality (i.e. in body, mind and spirit).

A brief overview has been included in respect to the various non-stipendiary possibilities for ordination within the Church of England, and this has been coupled with some statistics illustrating the growing crisis within the NHS in respect to the care of the elderly population and those with dementia. In direct response to the latter, an indication has been outlined as to how the Church might become more fully involved with healthcare, and where possible funding streams might come from to facilitate such work.

Finally, a radical proposition has been made for the training of candidates in the dual roles of physician

---

2014-2015 (Durham: The Department of Theology and Religion Durham University, 2014), p. 7. <https://www.dur.ac.uk/resources/theology.religion/postgrad/DThMHandbook2014-2015.pdf> [accessed 11 July 2015].

and priest, through partnership arrangements between theological and medical colleges, or by the innovative approach of a new theological-medical college, with people graduating as physician-priests in the truest sense.

Conclusion

After the priestly office, there is no profession that so commends itself to the heart of the humane as that of the Christian physician.[296]

Eliza Allen Starr

This dissertation was planned in order to examine, from Babylonian times onwards, the historically close relationship between priests and physicians, the subsequent development of the two separate professions of Church and Medicine, the role and association of the Church and the medical profession in later centuries, and the inter-relationship of the role of the two professions in the modern era (with specific reference to the specialities of general practice and psychiatry), concluding with an assessment as to whether there is a role for the 'physician-priest' in the 21st century.

In the introduction, reference was made to the concept that we are all spiritual beings, and that our humanness is secondary to that which is mystical within us. Attention was drawn to the recognised need for holistic care, which paradoxically exists against the backdrop of regulatory, anti-religious professional conformism

---

296 Starr, pp. 324–25.

despite the recognition that the physician (and especially the general practitioner) has largely replaced the priest in meeting the general needs of today's society.

Chapter One considered the historical, cultural and multi-faith perspectives of the priest-physician, demonstrating how the dual role was exercised by the same person for many centuries, transculturally and across most faiths.

Chapter Two took this exploration into the Christian era, examining how Jesus exercised a ministry that combined the roles of priest, teacher and physician, and how the importance of healing thus became central to early Christian theology. Attention was drawn to St Luke as the first Christian physician. Reflection was also made on how the Church of England had an early role in the appointment of physicians, and how it has rooted healing within its doctrine and liturgy.

In Chapter Three, modern-day perspectives and attitudes to the two roles of physician and priest were scrutinised, both from a layperson's viewpoint and from within the confines of professional medical regulation and the Anglican ordinal. It culminated in a reflection on how the two roles of priest and physician frequently overlap in practice, despite the exhortations of professional codes of practice to the contrary.

Finally, Chapter Four took a visionary journey into the future, attempting to build on certain germinating seeds that presently suggest a change of attitudes within the Church, the medical profession and society. It postulated how the Church and the world of healthcare

Conclusion

in general, and the NHS in particular, might have mutually beneficial aims and perspectives; with the possibility that central to all might be the re-emergence of the physician-priest.

The dissertation was given the title of 'The Healing Enigma'. An enigma can be both a paradox and a question. In this case, the paradox is provided by the fact that historically, as has been shown, people looked to the priests for help when they were sick. Regardless as to whether the problem was a physical ailment, a psychological illness, or a spiritual need, it was the priest-physician whose advice was sought in an attempt to bring about healing. However, in due course, it was the priests themselves who gradually decided that the practise of medicine was not an art in which priests ought to be involved. As a result, the medical profession was eventually born as a secular occupation, and priests were left to attend to spiritual matters only. As the centuries passed, the gap between medicine and the Church widened, until the situation extant within the 20th and early 21st centuries was reached, wherein the regulatory bodies for the medical and nursing professions have been seen to take disciplinary action against healthcare professionals over religious matters; giving rise to the general concept that there is no place for religion in the consulting room, despite the historical perspective. The inconsistency is widened by the expectation that, as a matter of good practice, physicians will, when treating their patients, take into consideration physical, psychological and social factors. In other words, physicians are expected to treat 'the whole person'. How this can be achieved without consideration of a person's spiritual and religious standing provides a contradiction that is yet to be satisfactorily resolved. To add to this perplexity, it is reasonable to say that the Church is not as involved in modern-day healthcare as it might be, despite the aforementioned unmet need, and by no means least of all, regardless of the irrefutable fact that Christianity is fundamentally a religion of healing. Ultimately, to call this an enigma is perhaps an understatement.

The inherent question following on from the above paradox is whether there is a resolution to be had that reduces this gulf between the two professions; a resolution that allows the Church to be more influential within the world of health care, and also allows appropriately minded physicians to be more overtly proactive in assisting their patients from a spiritual or religious perspective, where appropriate – especially in respect to illness whereby there is no known physical cure, but where healing in its purest form can still be achieved.

Hence, we have the 21st century healing enigma: there are great unmet healthcare needs within our communities; the NHS and statutory social services are unable to meet these needs and are unlikely to be able to do so within the foreseeable future; the Church is witnessing a demise in its popularity as a community hub; and the number of stipendiary priests within the Church of England is in marked decline. Ultimately, as Byrne wrote:

Conclusion

Good doctors and priests are made not only by their deep knowledge of medicine or theology, but also by their deep knowledge and love of the human soul and by their ability to communicate with another person.[297]

Taking all the above into account, there is a compelling argument for the Church to now restate its authority in respect to the matter of health care in general and healing in particular. The circumstances of the 21st century effectively offer an opportunity for the clock of history to be turned back on itself, thus allowing the timely, and arguably much needed, resurgence of the dually qualified physician-priest.

The possibilities are considerable if the willingness to pioneer and innovate exists. The next significant question is whether, as a senior member of the Establishment within the United Kingdom, and thus a leader within its field, the Church of England has the will, the foresight, the strength of purpose and the courage to become the primary mover in such a revolutionary transformation.

---

297 Kevin Byrne, 'Doctors one, priests one', *British Medical Journal*, 286 (1983), 1399–400.

Bibliography

Books

Bakan, David, Dan Merkur and David S. Weiss, *Maimonides' Cure of Souls: Medieval Precursor of Psychoanalysis* (New York: State University of New York Press, 2009).

Ball, Peter, *Anglican Spiritual Direction* (Harrisburg: Morehouse Publishing, 2007).

Ballard, Paul and John Pritchard, *Practical Theology in Action*, 2nd edn (London: SPCK, 2006).

Balsinger, Robert B., ed., The Westminster Assembly, *The Westminster Shorter Catechism with Proof Texts* (CreateSpace Independent Publishing Platform [1647] 2010).

Berlin, Adele and Marc Zvi Brettler, eds., *The Jewish Study Bible* (Oxford: Oxford University Press, 2004).

Bicknell, E. J., *A Theological Introduction to the Thirty-Nine Articles of the Church of England*, 3rd edn (Eugene: Wipf & Stock Publishers, 2007).

Boulton, David, *Who on Earth was Jesus?* (Winchester: O Books, 2008)

Bramley, H. R., trans., Gregory the Great, *On the Pastoral Charge* (Oxford: James Parker, 1874).

British Medical Association, *Divine Healing and Co-operation Between Doctors and Clergy* (London: British Medical Association, 1956).

Bynum, William, *The History of Medicine: A Very Short Introduction* (Oxford: Oxford University Press, 2008).

Cadbury, Henry J., *The Style and Literary Method of Luke* (Cambridge:

Harvard University Press, 1920).
Calder, R., *From Magic to Medicine* (London: Rathbone Books, 1957).
Carr, Wesley, *The Priestlike Task* (London: SPCK, 1985).
Cassell, Eric J., *The Healer's Art: A New Approach to the Doctor-Patient Relationship* (Harmondsworth: Penguin, 1978).
Church of England, *The Book of Common Prayer* (Oxford: Oxford University Press, [1662] 1969).
Cocksworth, Christopher and Rosalind Brown, *Being A Priest Today*, 2nd edn (Norwich: Canterbury Press, [2002] 2006).
Craik, Elizabeth M., *The Hippocratic Corpus: Content and Context* (London: Routledge, 2015).
Critchley, Macdonald, ed., *Butterworths Medical Dictionary*, 2nd edn (London: Butterworths, [1961] 1978).
Davie, Martin, *A Guide To The Church of England* (London: Bloomsbury, 2008).
Evans, C. F., *Saint Luke* (London: SCM Press, 1990).
Fry, Timothy, ed., *The Rule of St Benedict in English* (Collegeville: The Liturgical Press, 1981).
Furey, Robert J., *The Joy of Kindness* (New York: Crossroad Publishing Co., 1993).
General Medical Council, *Good Medical Practice* (London: General Medical Council, 2013).
Greaves, David, *The Healing Tradition: Reviving the soul of Western medicine* (Oxford: Radcliffe Publishing, 2004).
Grosseteste, Robert, *Templum Dei* (c.1219-1225), Joseph Goering and F.A.C. Mantello, eds., (Toronto: Pontifical Institute of Medieval Studies, 1984).
Harnack, Adolf von and William Douglas Morrison, *Luke the Physician: the Author of the Third Gospel and the Acts of ten Apostles* (London: Williams and Norgate, 1908).
Heyrman, J. and C. Spreeuwenbergh, eds., *Vocational training in general practice* (Leuven: Katholieke Universiteit Leuven, 1987).

Bibliography

Hobart, William Kirk, *The Medical Language of St Luke: A Proof from Internal Evidence That 'The Gospel According to St. Luke' and 'The Acts of the Apostles' Were Written by the Same Person, and That the Writer was a Medical Man* (Dublin: Hodges, Figgis & Co., 1882).

House of Bishops of the General Synod, *Eucharistic Presidency: A Theological Statement* (London: Church House Publishing, 1997).

Hugo, Victor, *Les Misérables* (London: Penguin Classics, [1862] 1982).

Jaggs-Fowler, Robert, *The Law and Medicine: Friend or Nemesis?* (London: Radcliffe Publishing, 2013).

Koenig, Harold G., Dana E. King and Verna Benner Carson, *Handbook of Religion and Health* 2nd edn (Oxford: Oxford University Press, 2012).

Kraemer, Joel L., *Maimonides: The Life and World of one of Civilisation's Greatest Minds* (New York: Doubleday Religion, 2010).

Larkin, Philip, *Collected Poems* (London and Boston: The Marvell Press and Faber and Faber, 1988).

Loewen, Peter, *Music in Early Franciscan Thought* (Leiden: Koninklijke Brill, 2013).

Macfarlane, Robert, *The Wild Places* (London: Granta Books, 2007).

Maddocks, Morris, *The Christian Healing Ministry*, 3rd edn (London: SPCK, [1981] 1995).

Maimonides, *The Guide of the Perplexed*, Chaim Rabin (trans.), (Indianapolis: Hackett Publishing Company, 1952).

Margotta, Roberto, *History of Medicine* (London: Octobus Publishing, [1996] 2001).

Marland, H. and M. Pelling, eds., *The Task of Healing: Medicine, Religion, and Gender in England and the Netherlands, 1450–1800* (Rotterdam: Erasmus Publishing, 1996).

Marshall, I. Howard, *Luke – Historian and Theologian* (Carlisle: Paternoster, 3rd edn. [1970] 1988).

McGrath, Alister E., *Christian Theology: An Introduction* (Chichester: Wiley-Blackwell, 2011).

Micklethwait, John and Adrian Wooldridge, *God is Back: How The Global Rise of Faith is Changing the World* (London: Penguin Books, 2009).

Nave, Orville J., ed., *Nave's Topical Bible* (Michigan: Zondervan, 1969).

Osler, William, *Aequanimita and Other Addresses* (London: H. K. Lewis, 1946).

Pattison, Stephen and James Woodward, *A Vision of Pastoral Theology* (Edinburgh: Contact Pastoral, 1994).

Pickering, Sue, *Spiritual Direction: A Practical Introduction* (Norwich: Canterbury Press, 2008).

Pollak, Kurt, *The Healers: The Doctor, Then and Now* (London: Thomas Nelson & Sons, 1963).

Porterfield, Amanda, *Healing in the History of Christianity* (Oxford: Oxford University Press, 2005).

Powell, Mark, *What Are They Saying About Luke?* (New York: Paulist Press, 1989).

Prioreschi, Plinio, *A History of Medicine* (Omaha: Horatius Press, 1995).

Ramsay, Michael, *The Christian Priest Today* (London: SPCK, 1972).

Rodwell, J. M., trans., *The Koran* (London: Phoenix, 1909).

Ruthven, Malise, *Islam: A Very Short Introduction* (Oxford: Oxford University Press, 2012).

Shapiro, Arthur K. and Elaine Shapiro, *The Powerful Placebo: From Ancient Priest to Modern Physician* (Baltimore: The John Hopkins University Press, 1997).

Smart, Ninian, *The World's Religions* (Cambridge: Cambridge University Press, 1989).

Soanes, Catherine, ed., *Compact Oxford English Dictionary*, 2nd edn (Oxford: Oxford University Press, 2000).

Starr, Eliza Allen, *Patron Saints* (Montana: Kessinger Publishing, [1883] 2003).

Strelan, Rick, *Luke the Priest: The Authority of the Author of the Third Gospel* (Aldershot: Ashgate, 2008).

Swinton, John, *Dementia: Living in the Memories of God* (Michigan: Eerdmans, 2012).

Taylor, Charles, *A Secular Age* (Cambridge, MA: Harvard University Press, 2007).

The Archbishops' Council, *A Time to Heal: The Development of Good Practice in the Healing Ministry: A Handbook* (London: Church House Publishing, 2000).

Common Worship: Services and Prayers for the Church of England: Ministry to the Sick (London: Church House Publishing, 2000).

Common Worship: Services and Prayers for the Church of England: Ordination Services (London: Church House Publishing, 2007).

The Canons of the Church of England, 7th edn (London: Church House Publishing, 2012).

The Holy Bible, New Revised Standard Version, Anglicized Edition (Oxford: Oxford University Press, 1995).

The Holy See, *Catechism of the Catholic Church*, 2nd edn (Citta del Vaticano: Libreria Editrice Vaticana, 2000).

Williams, Rowan, *A Ray of Darkness* (Cambridge MA: Cowley, 1995).

—*Being Christian* (London: SPCK, 2014).

Chapters and Articles in Books

Barry, F.R. 'The Case for Part Time Priests', in: Robin Denniston, ed., *Part Time Priests?* (London: Skeffington, 1960).

Bowden, John, 'Ministry and Ministers: Origins of the ordained ministry' in: John Bowden, ed., *Christianity: The Complete Guide* (London: Continuum, 2005).

Coleman, Mary E., 'John Calvin (1509–64)', in: Ian S. Markham, ed., *The Student's Companion to the Theologians* (Chichester: Wiley-Blackwell, 2013) 199–203.

Jowett, Benjamin, trans., 'The Dialogues of Plato: Charmides, or Temperance' (380BC) 156d3 – 157c6, in: Mortimer J. Adler, ed., *Great Books Vol. 6: Plato*, 2nd edn (Chicago: Encyclopaedia Britannica Inc., [1952] 1990).

Kearney, Michael and Radhule Weininger, 'Care of the soul', in: Mark Cobb, Christina M. Puchalski and Bruce Rumbold, eds., *Oxford Textbook of Spirituality in Healthcare* (Oxford: Oxford University Press, 2012).

Kirsch, Johann Peter, ed., 'Pope John XXI (XX)', in: *The Catholic Encyclopaedia* (New York: Robert Appleton Company, 1910), <http://www.newadvent.org/cathen/08429c.htm> [accessed 14 March 2015].

McGrath, Alister E., 'Christianity', in: Mark Cobb, Christina M. Puchalski and Bruce Rumbold, eds., *Oxford Textbook of Spirituality in Healthcare* (Oxford: Oxford University Press, 2012).

Powell, Andrew and Christopher MacKenna, 'Psychotherapy', in: Chris Cook, Andrew Powell and Christopher MacKenna, eds., *Spirituality and Psychiatry* (London: RCPsych Publications, 2009).

Rahman, F., 'Islam and Health/Medicine: A historical perspective', in: L. E. Sullivan, ed., *Healing and Restoring: Health and Medicine in the World's Religious Traditions* (New York: Macmillan Publishing Co., 1989).

Unnik, W. C. van, 'Luke-Acts, A Storm Center in Contemporary Scholarship', in: L. E. Keck and J. L. Martyn, eds., *Studies in Luke-Acts* (Nashville: Abingdon, 1966).

Journal Articles

Alphonse Karr, Jean-Baptiste, *Les Guêpes*, vol. vi. (Paris: Société Belge de librairie, Jan 1849).

Barnard, David, 'The Physician as Priest, Revisited', *Journal of Religion and Health*, 24, 4 (1985), 272–86.

Bibliography

Been, Wouter de and Sanne Taekema, 'Religion in the 21st Century: Debating the Post-Secular Turn', *Erasmus Law Review*, 5, no. 1 (2012), 1–3.

Byrne, Kevin, 'Doctors one, priests one', *British Medical Journal*, 286 (1983), 1399–400.

Chattopadhyay, S., 'Religion, spirituality, health and medicine: Why should Indian physicians care?', *Journal of Postgraduate Medicine*, 53, no. 4 (2007), 262–6.

Constantelos, Demetrios J., 'Physician-Priests in the Medieval Greek Church', *Greek Orthodox Theological Review*, 11 (1966), 141–53.

Coury, Charles, 'The Basic Principles of Medicine in the Primitive Mind', *Medical History*, 11 (1967), 111–27.

Drott, Edward R., 'Gods, Buddhas, and Organs: Buddhist Physicians and Theories of Longevity in Early Medieval Japan', *Japanese Journal of Religious Studies*, 37, no. 2 (2010), 247–73.

Dyer, Clare, 'GP is struck off for imposing his religious views on a vulnerable patient', *BMJ*, 350 (2015), 4.

Guerra, Francisco, 'Maya Medicine', *Medical History*, 8 (1964), 31–43.

Hamarneh, Sami, 'Development of Hospitals in Islam', *Journal of the History of Medicine and Allied Sciences*, 17, no. 3 (1962), 366–84.

Hyman, Arthur, 'Maimonides' "Thirteen Principles"', *Jewish Medieval and Renaissance Studies*, (1967), 119–144.

Jain, S. and P. N. Tandon, 'Ayurvedic medicine and Indian literature on epilepsy', *Neurology Asia*, 9, Supplement 1 (2004), 57–8.

Knight, James A., 'The Minister as Healer, the Healer as Minister', *Journal of Religion and Health*, 21, 2 (1982), 101.

Majeed, Azeem, 'How Islam changed medicine', *BMJ*, 331 (2005), 1486–7.

Olesen, Frede, Jim Dickinson and Per Hjortdahl, 'General practice — time for a new definition', *BMJ*, 320 (2000), 354–7.

Padela, Aasim I. and others, 'Health: Perspectives of Muslim Community Leaders in Southeast Michigan', *Journal of Religion and Health*, 50, no. 2 (2011), 359–73.

Pink, Jim Lionel Jacobson and Mike Pritchard, 'The 21st century GP: physician and priest?', *British Journal of General Practice*, 57, 543 (2007), 840–43.

Scott, Edward M., 'Combining the Roles of "Priest" and "Physician": A Clinical Case', *Journal of Religion and Health*, 18, 2 (1979), 160–3.

Shapiro, Johanna, 'Knowing What a Human Life Really Is: Doctors and Priests', *Family Medicine* 32, 9 (2000), 598–9.

Sims, A. C. P., 'The Psychiatrist as Priest', *Journal of the Royal Society of Health*, 5 (1988), 160–3.

Taavoni, S., 'Only a nice man can be a nice physician', *Iran Journal of Nursing*, 13, no. 21 (1999), 42–5.

Tourle, Colin, 'Peter Wallis: Anglican priest and former general practitioner', *BMJ*, 349 (2014), 25.

Vernesi, Cristiano and others, 'Genetic characterization of the body attributed to the evangelist Luke', *Proceedings of the National Academy of Sciences of the USA*, 98 (2001), 13460–3.

Welch, John S., 'Ritual in Western Medicine and Its Role in Placebo Healing', *Journal of Religion and Health*, 42, no. 1 (2003), 21–33.

Wenham, John, 'The Identification of Luke', *The Evangelical Quarterly*, 63, no. 1 (1991), 3–44.

Wexler, Leonard, 'The Prayer of Maimonides', *Oncology Times*, 31, no. 4 (2009), 3.

The Bible

Old Testament
Leviticus 11.16.
Deuteronomy 18.14–22.
Isaiah 49.15–16.
Psalm 2; 110.1–4.

New Testament

Matthew 9.35; 10.1; 12.9–13; 20.29–34; 21.11.
Mark 1.24, 40–42; 2.8–12; 2.17; 3.5; 5.41; 6.56; 9.17–18; 10.17–22.
Luke 4.23, 24; 9.1–6; 22.49-51; 24.13–32.
John 3.1–21; 5.1–16; 18.36.
Acts 8.32–35; 11.2; 28.10.
Colossians 1.21–22; 4.14.
Ephesians 4.1–13.
Hebrews 7.25; 9.12, 24.
1 Peter 5.1–2.

UK Statutes (Acts of Parliament)

Ecclesiastical Licences Act 1533.
Health and Social Care Act 2012.
Peter's Pence Act 1533.

Reports and Documents

Alzheimer's Disease International, *World Alzheimer's Report 2014: Dementia and Risk Reduction – an analysis of protective and modifiable factors* (London: Alzheimer's Disease International, 2014), <http://www.alz.co.uk/research/world-report-2014> [accessed 20 June 2015].

Archbishops' Council, *Church Statistics 2010/11: Parochial attendance, membership and finance statistics together with statistics of licensed ministers for the Church of England, January to December* (London: Archbishops' Council Research and Statistics, Central Secretariat, 2012).

Department of Health, *Prime Minister's challenge on dementia 2020* (London: Department of Health, 2015).

Department of Health and Department for Communities and Local Government, *Better Care Fund 2015/2016: Policy Framework*, <https://www.gov.uk/government/uploads/system/uploads/attachment_data/file/381848/BCF.pdf> [accessed 20 June 2015].

General Medical Council, *Good Medical Practice* (London: General Medical Council, 2013).

Finlay of Llandaff, Ilora, (Chair), *Guiding Patients Through Complexity: Modern Medical Generalism* (London: The Royal College of General Practitioners and The Health Foundation, 2011), <http://www.health.org.uk/public/cms/75/76/4299/2763/COMMISSION%20REPORT%20ON%20MEDICAL%20GENERALISM%20OCTOBER%202011.pdf?realName=xbuUe5.pdf> [accessed 24 May 2015].

NHS England, *NHS England Standard Alternative Provider Medical Services Contract 2014/2015*, <http://www.england.nhs.uk/wp-content/uploads/2014/06/apms-standard-contract-june14.pdf> [accessed 20 June 2015].

Office for National Statistics, *2011 Census*.

World Health Organisation, *Constitution of the World Health Organisation* (New York: World Health Organisation, 1946), <http://apps.who.int/gb/bd/PDF/bd47/EN/constitution-enpdf> [accessed 28 April 2015].

World Health Organisation, *The World Health Report 2001: Mental Health – New Understanding, New Hope* (Geneva: WHO, 2001).

Internet Articles

About Health, *What is Mental Health?*, <http://mentalhealth.about.com/cs/stressmanagement/a/whatismental.ht> [accessed 4 June 2015].

Bole, William, 'Jesuit MDs: Walking with Ignatius on Their

Bibliography

Medical Rounds', *Jesuits*, 2010, 12–13, <http://www.sjnen.org/Document.Doc?id=39> [accessed 07 June 2015].

Buhler, G. (trans.), 'Manusmrti: The Laws of Manu', <http://sanskritdocuments.org/all_pdf/manusmriti.pdf> [accessed 07 March 2015].

Calvin, John, *The Institutes of the Christian Religion* (1536) Bk. II, Chp. 15, p. 305, tran. by Henry Beveridge, <http://www.ntslibrary.com/PDF%20Books/Calvin%20Institutes%20of%20Christian%20Religion.pdf> [accessed 11 April 2015].

Damascenos, John, *De Fide Orthodoxa*, Bk.II, ch. XII (650-754 AD), <http://www.documentacatholicaomnia.eu/03d/0675-0749,_Ioannes_Damascenus,_De_Fide_Orthodoxa,_EN.pdf> [accessed 13 March 2015].

Department of Health, *A Short Guide to Health and Wellbeing Boards*, <http://webarchive.nationalarchives.gov.uk/20130805112926/http://healthandcare.dh.gov.uk/hwb-guide/> [accessed 20 June 2015].

Department of Theology, *Doctor of Theology and Ministry Handbook 2014-2015* (Durham: The Department of Theology and Religion Durham University, 2014), <https://www.dur.ac.uk/resources/theology.religion/postgrad/DThMHandbook2014-2015.pdf> [accessed 11 July 2015].

Editorial, 'Doctor-Turned-Priest Makes Villages in Southern India "Blood Literate"', (*UCA-News.com*, 09 June 2004), <http://www.ucanews.com/storyarchive/?post_name=/2004/06/09/doctorturnedpriest-makes-villages-in-southern-india-blood-literate&post_id=24280> [accessed 07 June 2015].

Editorial, 'Doctor's Visit Nets New Parish Priest', (*The Church of the GOC of America*, 07 February 2013), <http://www.hotca.org/parishes/417-doctors-visit-nets-new-parish-priest> [accessed 07 June 2015].

Eusebius, *Ecclesiastical History* (circa 340 AD) Bk. 1, Chp. 3, Para. 8

<http://www.documentacatholicaomnia.eu/03d/0265-0339,_Eusebius_Caesariensis,_Church_History,_EN.pdf> [accessed 1 April 2015].

General Medical Council, 'Dr Richard Scott Investigation Committee decision', 14 June 2012 <http://www.gmc-uk.org/news/13333.asp> [accessed 05 August 2015].

Gharzeddine, Omar, 'Italian Priest and Medical Doctor, American NGO, Win 2014 United Nations Population Award', (*United Nations Population Fund*, 21 March 2014), <http://www.unfpa.org/news/italian-priest-and-medical-doctor-american-ngo-win-2014-united-nations-population-award> [accessed 07 June 2015].

Hunt, Jeremy, *New Deal for General Practice* (London: Department of Health, 2015), <https://www.gov.uk/government/speeches/new-deal-for-general-practice> [accessed 20 June 2015].

Lambeth Palace Library, *Lambeth Palace Library Research Guide: Medical Licences Issued by the Archbishop of Canterbury 1535-1775*, 2. <www.lambethpalacelibrary.org/files/Medical_Licences.pdf> [accessed 26 April 2015].

Living Faith Forum, *The Pentecostal Doctrine of Healing*, New Beginning Christian Ministries, <http://livingfaithforum.org/healing.html> [accessed 02 May 2015].

Mansi, Joannes Dominicus, *Sacrorum Conciliorum Nova et Amplissima Collectio*, vol. 2 (1692-1769) col. 693D, <http://www.documentacatholicaomnia.eu/01_50_1692-1769-_Mansi_JD.html> [accessed 13 March 2015]

MentalHealth.gov, *What is Mental Health?* < http://www.mentalhealth.gov/basics/what-is-mental-health/> [accessed 04 June 2015].

Needle, Paul, CPAS Resource Sheet 9: *Ministers in Secular Employment*, <http://www.cpas.org.uk/download/1204/web_upload%252F9%2BSecularEmployment%2BRS09-single-1268750864.pdf> [accessed 10 June 2015].

Bibliography

NHS, *NHS Careers: General Practice*, <http://www.nhscareers.nhs.uk/explore-by-career/doctors/careers-in-medicine/general-practice/> [accessed 3 June 2015].

NHS, *NHS Careers: Psychiatry*, <http://www.nhscareers.nhs.uk/explore-by-career/doctors/careers-in-medicine/psychiatry/> [accessed 3 June 2015].

NHS England, *Better Care Fund Planning*, <http://www.england.nhs.uk/ourwork/part-rel/transformation-fund/bcf-plan/> [accessed 20 June 2015].

Office for National Statistics, *Religious Affiliation, England and Wales, 2011*, < http://www.ons.gov.uk/ons/rel/census/2011-census/key-statistics-for-local-authorities-in-england-and-wales/styreligion.html> [accessed 05 June 2015].

Palmo, Rocco, 'Jesuit, Priest, Physician, "Rock Star"', *(Whispers in the Loggia*, 16 August 2006), <http://whispersintheloggia.blogspot.co.uk/2006/08/jesuit-priest-physician-rock-star.html> [accessed 07 June 2015].

Sidersky, Robyn, 'Doctor-turned-priest faces new challenge to overcome: learning to walk again' (*The Patriot News*, 19 January 2011), <http://www.pennlive.com/midstate/index.ssf/2011/01/doctor-turned-priest_faces_new.html> [accessed 07 June 2015].

Sīnā, Ibn (Avicenna), *Al-Qānūn fī al-Ṭibb (The Canon of Medicine)* (c. 1025), <http://archive.org/stream/AvicennasCanonOfMedicine/9670940-Canon-of-Medicine_djvu.txt> [accessed 30 March 2015].

The Church of England, *Exploring Pioneer Ministry: A Short Guide*, 2. <https://www.freshexpressions.org.uk/sites/default/files/ExploringPioneerMinistry_2.pdf> [accessed 20 June 2015].

Zysk, Kenneth, 'Mythology and the brahmanization of Indian medicine: transforming heterodoxy into orthodoxy', www.hindu.dk, <http://www.hindu.dk/4/ar/zysk2.pdf> [accessed 07 March 2015].

Internet Sites

Army, *Funding Support: Medical Services bursary*, <http://www.army.mod.uk/training_education/25683.aspx> [accessed 20 June 2015].

Bishop Grosseteste University, <http://www.bishopg.ac.uk/Pages/default.aspx> [accessed 20 June 2015].

Creighton University School of Medicine, <http://medschool.creighton.edu/> [accessed 04 July 2015].

Diocese of Lincoln, *Lincoln School of Theology*, <http://www.lincoln.anglican.org/education-training/lincoln-school-of-theology/> [accessed 20 June 2015].

Diocese of Lincoln, *Spiritual Direction: Companions on the Way*, <http://www.lincoln.anglican.org/resources-parishes-ministry/spirituality/spiritual-direction/> [accessed 04 July 2015].

Durham University, *Profiles: Professor Chris Cook*, <https://www.dur.ac.uk/theology.religion/staff/profile/?id=3700> [accessed 07 June 2015].

Fresh Expressions, <https://www.freshexpressions.org.uk/> [accessed 12 June 2015].

Georgetown University School of Medicine, <https://som.georgetown.edu/> [accessed 04 July 2015].

Hull York Medical School, <http://www.hyms.ac.uk/> [accessed 20 June 2015].

Loyola University, Stritch School of Medicine, <http://ssom.luc.edu/> [accessed 04 July 2015].

Saint Louis University School of Medicine, <http://www.slu.edu/medicine> [accessed 04 July 2015].

St Hugh's Church, Old Brumby, North Lincolnshire, <https://www.facebook.com/pages/St-Hughs-Church-Old-Brumby/412046958915218?sk=timeline&ref=page_internal> [accessed 07 June 2015].

Bibliography

The Church of England, *Pioneer Ministry*, <https://www.churchofengland.org/clergy-office-holders/ministry/selection/pioneer-ministry.aspx> [accessed 12 June 2015].

The Jesuits, <http://jesuits.org/aboutus> [04 July 2015].

University of Lincoln, <http://www.lincoln.ac.uk/home/> [accessed 20 June 2015].

Newspaper & Media Reports

BBC, 'Faith row Margate GP Richard Scott gets formal warning', *BBC News Kent*, 14 June 2012, < http://www.bbc.co.uk/news/uk-england-kent-18445924> [accessed 23 May 2015].

Bingham, John, 'Christianity now written off as fixation with 'sky pixie' – Michael Gove', *Telegraph*, 01 April 2015, <http://www.telegraph.co.uk/news/religion/11510368/Christianity-now-written-off-as-fixation-with-sky-pixie-Michael-Gove.html> [accessed 23 May 2015].

Cohen, Nick, 'Secular Britain is ruled by religious bureaucrats', *Guardian*, 16 December 2012, <http://www.theguardian.com/commentisfree/2012/dec/16/secular-britain-ruled-by-religious-bureaucrats> [accessed 25 May 2015].

Hammond, Laura, 'Doctor turned Vicar takes on new role at Burton churches', *Burton Mail*, 12 December 2014, <http://www.burtonmail.co.uk/Doctor-turned-vicar-takes-new-role-Burton/story-22800557-detail/story.html> [accessed 07 June 2015].

Hargett, Malea, 'Former Arkansan provides healing as a priest and doctor', *Arkansas Catholic*, 28 October 2006, <http://www.arkansas-catholic.org/news/article/675> [accessed 07 June 2015].

Parris, Matthew, 'GPs will soothe you, but won't really cure you', *The Times*, 15th September 2012, <http://www.thetimes.co.uk/

tto/opinion/columnists/matthewparris/article3538931.ece>
[accessed 25 May 2015].

Shakespeare, John, 'Philip Larkin: An Extraordinary Series of Letters from Philip Larkin to John Shakespeare', *Telegraph*, 23 April 2009, <http://www.telegraph.co.uk/culture/books/bookreviews/5207870/Philip-Larkin.html> [accessed 06 June 2015].

Wade, Nicholas, 'Body of St Luke Gains Credibility', *New York Times*, 16th October, 2001, < http://www.nytimes.com/2001/10/16/world/body-of-st-luke-gains-credibility.html> [accessed 19 April 2015].

Ward, Lucy, 'Una Kroll: "Public protest is still very important"', *Guardian*, 17 November 2014, <http://www.theguardian.com/lifeandstyle/2014/nov/17/una-kroll-nun-doctor-priest-women-interview> [accessed 07 June 2015].

Winerip, Michael, 'When A Physician Becomes A Priest', *New York Times*, 29 May 1986, <http://articles.sun-sentinel.com/1986-05-29/features/8602010910_1_monk-new-priest-roman-catholic-priest> [accessed 07 June 2015].

Woodhead, Linda, 'Not enough boots on the ground', *Church Times*, 07 February 2014, <http://www.churchtimes.co.uk/articles/2014/7-february/features/features/not-enough-boots-on-the-ground> [accessed 10 June 2015].

Wyatt, Tim 'C of E attendance statistics slope still points downward', *Church Times*, 14 November 2014, <http://www.churchtimes.co.uk/articles/2014/14-november/news/uk/c-of-e-attendance-statistics-slope-still-points-downward> [accessed 05 June 2015].

Miscellaneous Papers

Cox, John, 'Doctors, Clergy and the troubled Soul: two professions, one vocation?' Royal College of Psychiatrists, Spirituality and Psychiatry Special Interest Group, Newsletter 32, 2011. <http://www.gohealth.org.uk/Report%20on%20SPSIG%20 meeting%202.11.11.%20Cox.pdf> [accessed 05 June 2015].

Personal Correspondence

Amin, Ibrahim (Imam), Oxford Centre for Islamic Studies, University of Oxford, personal correspondence, March 2015.

Ballantyne, Jenny, GP, North Thoresby, Lincolnshire, personal correspondence, 16 May 2015.

Foster, Peter (Geneticist), Cambridge, personal correspondence, December 2011.